How to Sell More Than 75% of Your Freelance Writing

Gordon Burgett

Prima Publishing & Communications
P.O. Box 1260B1
Rocklin, CA 95677
(916) 624-5718

Typography by Howarth & Smith Limited
Copyediting by Anne Montague
Production by Rosaleen Bertolino, Bookman Productions
Interior design by Judith Levinson
Cover design by The Dunlavey Studio

Prima Publishing & Communications
Rocklin, CA

Library of Congress Cataloging-in-Publication Data

Burgett, Gordon, 1938-
   How to sell more than 75% of your freelance writing /
     Gordon Burgett.   p.   cm.
   Reprint. Originally published: 1st ed. Carpinteria, CA:
     Write to Sell. c1984.

   ISBN 1-55958-035-6

   1. Authorship—Marketing.   2. Queries
(Authorship).   I. Title.
     II. Title: How to sell seventy-five percent of your freelance
     writing.
[PN161.B79   1990]
808'.02—dc20   89-48544   CIP

90 91 92 93   RRD   10 9 8 7 6 5 4 3 2 1

Printed in the United States of America

DEDICATION

To *Bill*, who has been ordained since the first edition of this book. He will always be successful with whichever flock he tends. Nice to have a twin with divine clout;

To *Jim*, my "kid brother," now a superintendent of schools, whose decency, wit, and concern about others will always distinguish him in education and life;

To *Nancy*, always my little sister, whose boundless energy and creative accomplishments in music and drama, and soon in writing, make a difference in the lives of those she touches;

To *Thelma*, "Mumsie," who is aging gracefully and threatening to outlive the reprints of all my books, in print and planned;

To *Virgil*, posthumously, now, one hopes, with more time to bowl, golf, garden, and read;

To *Judy*, still a Burgett but free;

To *Shannon* and *Kimberley*, diplomaed in part from the proceeds of the first edition of this book, always the pride of their gloating father, and

To *nieces and nephews*—Debbie, Bob, Tom, John, Stacy, Jennifer, Doug, and Brandon. What a group, not a lout in the lot, who beget even more Burgetts, to infect America for centuries to come. If they want to get into print for pay, I hope this book helps them too.

Special thanks to Hannah Sampson and Patricia Allaback for their priceless editorial assistance and encouragement.

CONTENTS

INTRODUCTION

When I was a beginner I would have laughed at the suggestion that I could sell 75% of my writing. In fact, I couldn't sell 5%. And what I did sell was to markets paying a few pennies a word, on publication.

The problem wasn't the writing—that was acceptable. I didn't know how to approach the editor or how to find a topic that he or she needed. But I accepted my dismal sales ratio. After all, aren't beginners supposed to suffer?

Wrong! Beginners are supposed to learn—and to begin.

But where is it written that you shouldn't earn a satisfactory return on your time and effort while you learn? And that you shouldn't be in print regularly from the start? Isn't that the purpose? So let me provide the steps and the rationale for the earning while you provide the beginning and the learning!

Don't laugh at the prospect of selling three of every four items you write. Professionals top that ratio daily. I'm going to show you how you can too, starting now. There's not a one of you, given literacy and persistence, who can't do it—if you will put in the effort. I would have saved a decade of doubt and unprinted production had I read and followed this book when I began. But no such book existed. You are luckier: you have it in hand!

Still, the book isn't an abracadabra that will magically put you in print. There is no such magic. It works only if you do. This book explains a profes-

sional system of selling, then writing. Success comes
from applying that system.

*How to Sell More Than 75% of Your Freelance
Writing* is a "how-to" book based on three simple
premises: (1) It's not hard to sell what you write. (2)
You can be in print and paid well for your writing
just about as quickly as you find a salable topic and
follow the steps in this book. (3) The amount of material you sell will be directly determined by how much
effort and skill you put into its preparation and sale.

Most beginners think that 90% of publishing success comes from the writing, from some creative or
mystical word order. Undeniably, literacy, clarity in
expression, accuracy, and a basic readability of the
copy are important. Yet the "best" writer alive may
never be published. Most of the lasting success comes
from selling the idea and copy.

Like riding a bicycle or swimming, writing is learn-
able and gets better with the doing. But most writers
do less and less of it if they don't sell early and often.
So the emphasis in this book is on the selling from the
outset.

It focuses on the hows of putting your ideas and
words in somebody else's publication for a profit.
Mostly it talks about process. In the background,
though close to the surface, will be money. Fame is
left to fate.

HOW THIS BOOK CAN HELP

First we will look at the many forms of writing that
freelancers sell. Those will be divided into two
groups: high-risk and low-risk, with risk being the
time it takes to prepare and sell an item in each category. Since most can regularly sell more than 75% of

submissions only in the low-risk category, this book will focus there.

Two kinds of writing where a 75% sales rate can be regularly attained and sustained are (1) queried non-fiction articles (and books) and (2) simultaneous submissions.

A formula is then offered that shows how each of these categories can yield that sales rate. It also suggests that in those categories 75% is quite modest, and that professionals regularly sell more than 100% of what they write in (1) and (2), through reprints, rewrites, and other means of multiple sales.

Six factors are then presented that will serve as the organizational structure for much of the rest of the book, since each further explains how that sales ratio is met while at the same time defining the process.

The selling/writing process is summarized in a chart and a guide. Figure 2, "The Mechanics of Getting Into Print," shows graphically how low-risk, queried items differ from higher-risk, direct submissions. Figure 3, "How to Prepare and Market Articles that Sell," outlines the 15 steps that queried nonfiction articles follow from inception to sale, and explains how simultaneous submissions differ.

Five elements from "How to Prepare and Market Articles That Sell" are then explained in greater detail:

"Picking and Defining a Topic"

"The Feasibility Study"

"Writing the Query Letter"

"Responding to the Replies"

"Researching, Writing, and Mailing"

An additional chapter, "Rights: Copyrights and Other

Rights," is inserted where an explanation is most appropriate.

So you go from an idea to a printed article. And beyond. There's a better way to do what we have learned, to multiply the one-idea, one-sale approach, called "topic-spoking": how to turn one idea into many manuscripts and thousands of dollars more in sales.

Another means of multiplying the sales income is by reselling the same copy again and again, so "Reselling the Sales" discusses reprints, rewrites, modified reprints, mixed markets, and sales abroad.

Chapter 11 explains how writing expenses can result in tax savings. In the final chapter a workbook, described in "Book Idea," is suggested as a place to capture and preserve good ideas for future use.

The nice thing about this method is that you can follow it as you wish: daily, when the muse inspires, or all the time.

WHO AM I TO TELL YOU HOW TO WRITE AND SELL?

I'm you 35 years later. In the beginning I knew nothing about writing, had never met a paid writer, and had nothing more in my skills bag than literacy and tenacity.

It turned out that they were enough, that volume and doggedness overwhelmed the folly of my sales approach. I did what I tell you not to do—for years. Wrote things and sent them in. A few sold. (The $4 I received for my first sale, a juvenile fiction piece called "Piedras Blancas," was devoured at a celebration supper that night!) So why should you do what I say?

Because now I've had more than 1,000 items in

print, about half in major magazines and top newspapers. And because it's been some years since I haven't sold far more than 100% of what I wrote. Most important, because I've taken the hard-learned lessons of my own past, devised a system that works, and compared it to what other professionals do. The biggest surprise: We all do just about the same thing! Which is what I'm sharing with you on these pages.

Where have I been in print? Almost everywhere but scripts. The list runs from *The Runner* to *Better Homes and Gardens* to *Jack and Jill* to *The Rotarian* to *Modern Bride* to *Dynamic Years*, and continues running. On the newspaper side, sports for the hometown papers was my teething ground, two newspaper editorships followed early on, then many a travel piece in the *Washington Post, Chicago Tribune, Newsday, L.A. Times, Boston Globe, Toronto Star,* and scores more.

I've sold comedy greeting cards by the pound (to Hallmark, Gibson, Joli, and others), edited six books, published eight more, appeared in several, and have written *The Query Book* (1980), *Ten Sales from One Article Idea: The Process and Correspondence* (1981), the first edition of this book in 1984, *Speaking for Money* (with Mike Frank) in 1985, *Query Letters/ Cover Letters: How They Sell Your Writing* (1985), *Empire-Building by Writing and Speaking* (1987), and *Self-Publishing to Tightly-Targeted Markets* (1989).

Perhaps most important, the topic of this book has been the heart of a four-hour seminar, the core of an annual 110-seminar schedule since 1981. It began as a communications class at California State University, Dominguez Hills, when I was the evening administrator in the '70s, and spawned so much interest that I left that position to lecture extensively on the topic of selling one's writing.

There's more, but what is important here is this: I've done many times everything that I suggest to you. It has worked for me, works regularly for other professionals, and has helped literally thousands who attended my seminars get into print. This book is the bread-and-butter stuff that can bring you more of both.

THE REASON TO WRITE

Beyond the writing and the selling, I see this book in terms of hope and dreams without which our lives would be, if not nearly pointless, at least much harder. Central to the dreams of many is the hope of leaving something of themselves on earth, a contribution or at least a mark on the pages of history. Yet few are as gifted as, say, Mozart or Picasso or Shakespeare. Most of us are of more common clay.

Still, the universe is made of lesser stars too, and written works in print, paid for and thus validated at least commercially, have their own levels of distinction, permanence, and even brilliance.

Just as important, something of each writer shines through. A thought, an idea, the sharing of an experience, the telling of a why and what and how enrich the world, and gain in value as they pass from the written to the oral and mental experience of others.

Something of yours in print is a fleck of immortality, an extension of you when your earthly time expires. Those words are records of your having creatively existed, a tangible something to be read and shared with your great-grandchildren's great-grandchildren.

That is a dream, and a worthy dream. So more than just filling your pockets with coins and paper with words, I particularly hope that this book will help make your dream of being in print, for whatever reason, a reality.

ADDITIONAL THOUGHTS

The term *nonfiction articles* is a redundancy, of course. There are no fiction articles; that is, all articles are nonfiction or are supposed to be. But I join the terms here to remind me and you that we are talking about articles *and* nonfiction, that both elements must be kept in mind.

With little deviation I refer to writers and editors as males in this text, though I know full well that many of each, perhaps even a majority, are women. Also, that literary and writing skills know no gender. Why do I do it? Ignorance? To twist the lioness's tail? Chauvinism? Nothing that complex. Because "he/she" and like contrivances read and sound goofy and because historically "he" has meant "person" in a collective sense. So, at the risk of feminist rage, I bow to history.

How to Order:

Quantity discounts are available from the publisher, Prima Publishing & Communications, P.O. Box 1260B1, Rocklin, CA 95677; telephone (916) 624-5718. On your letterhead include information concerning the intended use of the books and the number of books you wish to purchase.

U.S. Bookstores and Libraries: Please submit all orders to St. Martin's Press, 175 Fifth Avenue, New York, NY 10010; telephone (212) 674-5151.

PART ONE

The Process

CHAPTER 1

Low-Risk Versus High-Risk Writing

There are only two areas in the freelance writing field where you can consistently sell 75% of what you produce and submit. A review of the forms of freelancing will show how those two were selected.

Figure 1 on page 4 shows the kinds of writing most frequently engaged in by freelancers and divides them into two distinct categories: *low-risk* (where you can regularly expect to sell 75% or more of what you write) and *high-risk* (where that selling ratio would be highly unlikely).

Risk in this case is the time it takes to prepare and sell an item in that category. Defining by risk doesn't pass judgment on the forms of writing, on the artistic merit or difficulty of creation in the various fields, nor on the amount of money one can earn in each field.

This chart attempts to measure the relative sales risk of various forms of writing/selling. It does not pass judgment on the merits of the forms nor suggest which is the most lucrative. It shows where the greatest number of sales might occur should a writer offer the same number of items (in final selling form) for

Figure 1 Selling Risk

Low Risk	A. NONFICTION QUERIED SUBMISSIONS	articles books
	B. NONFICTION SIMULTANEOUS SUBMISSIONS	newspaper travel newspaper weekly supplements religious regional in-flights
Line of demarcation between types of writing/selling where the writer can reasonably expect to sell more than 75% of what he writes.		
High Risk	C. NONFICTION UNQUERIED SUBMISSIONS	humor other nonfiction markets
	D. GREETING CARDS	
	E. SCRIPTS	TV/radio movie stage
	F. FICTION	short stories books
	G. POETRY	

sale in each field. (It includes the possibility of selling the same item more than once.) Thus the greater the potential sales, the lower the risk.

    A. NONFICTION QUERIED: Since you write only when you have a go-ahead in reply to a query, and can rewrite and reprint after the sale(s), you should be able to sell more than 100% of what you write.

B. NONFICTION SIMULTANEOUS SUBMIS-SIONS: Although you must write and send the manuscript unsolicited, you can send many copies of the same piece at the same time. The pay range is lower here but you can maintain a high selling ratio.

C. NONFICTION UNQUERIED SUBMISSIONS: The beginners' system: Get an idea, write it, send it. With great writing, ideas, and patience, you might sell 20% of what you submit. The difference is the query.

D. GREETING CARDS: While your percentage will always be low (selling 1 of 12, in a batch, is super!), a writer with a sense of humor turning out volume can make money here. Highly competitive.

E. SCRIPTS: Usually requires writing and writing until you "sell" an agent, then doing it again until you have a salable script. A lot of writing, at least in the beginning. Yet the pay range makes it worthwhile.

F. FICTION: Selling short stories is a lost art, and "first" books are more often the third or seventh written, so the percentage of selling what you actually write is low. Sadly, except for the rare blockbusters, the pay on a per-hour basis is also low when you finally do sell.

G. POETRY: The only bread to be had from poetry is in the bread line.

After looking quickly at the high-risk group, we will concentrate on (A) *nonfiction queried submissions* (articles and books), and (B) *nonfiction simultaneous submissions*, where you can expect to sell at the 75% level from the beginning, regularly, and for as long as you continue to follow the formula and produce salable copy.

HIGH-RISK FORMS OF WRITING

It's also possible that in (C) humor writing, (E) scripts, and (F) fiction, you could sell more than 75% of what you write, but it would be close to a miracle if that occurred from the outset. In all three areas you normally write reams of material before sales become regular, your name becomes known, and your output is sought and bought with much consistency.

While (C) through (G) aren't ranked in any order, few would deny that (G) *poetry* would be the hardest from which to eke a living. It is the true path to penury. The ratio of poems bought to those composed is painfully small. A 75% sales rate from poetry is so far from reality only a poet could imagine it.

The tongue-twisting category of nonfiction nonqueried single submissions, (C), includes *unsolicited submissions*. This is where beginners usually start, and is the source of much frustration and many needless letters of rejection. We will discuss it more fully later. For now, with extraordinary luck and good writing you might sell 20% of your unsolicited submissions, almost all to low-paying, pay-on-publication magazines. Five percent is more likely.

Humor also belongs in (C). The larger field of "humor" is divided into two types, one in this category and the other in the low-risk (A). The humor of (C) is the *Mad* magazine variety, or the gems penned by Erma Bombeck and Woody Allen. They are written to be funny. Humor is their purpose; the subject is simply a vehicle for a laugh. And they're hard to sell because they can't be queried.

What would you say? "Editor: Would you like to read something so funny it will knock you off your stool?" To which the editor, firmly seated, can only reply, "Sure, send it. Let's see if it makes me laugh!"

So humor pieces must be sent unsolicited, hence unexpected, which is guaranteed to keep their sales ratio and paying price low.

Fortunately, most magazine humor pieces don't fall into the pure humor (C) category. They are "humorous" and can be queried, humorously, so they belong in (A). They have a purpose—the topic is being written about for a reason—and humor is the style. They are articles written humorously. And since they can be queried before being written, they can be sold at better than a 75% ratio.

Greeting cards (D) will never be a 75% category unless you are publishing them yourself. If you sell 1 sentiment from a submitted batch of perhaps 12, for a sales ratio of 8.5%, that's good. Still, humor lines (without art) pay well, so a writer with a sense of humor and persistence who submits in volume can make money in this highly competitive field.

The best money may be in scriptwriting, with television scripts currently in the lead. But the number of scripts usually written before a sale is made, plus the amount of rewriting later, keep *scripts* (E) in the high-risk category for most writers as long as they write.

Fiction (F) may be the riskiest of all. Selling short stories to a badly eroded market rivals poetry for sheer difficulty. Some say it is harder to sell short stories than novels, which in itself is no easy task. In both cases it takes weeks or months—sometimes years—of writing to produce an item for sale. No querying, no assurance, nothing but hope and typing, usually with very little pay at the other end for all but the few whose six-digit advances stand in stark contrast to the reality of the average fiction writer's income.

A word or two before backtracking to (A) and (B). Because (C) through (G) generally pay low and slow, and sales follow much on-faith writing, is no reason any or all of these categories shouldn't be ardently pursued. Nor is it to say that nonfiction articles, (A), are somehow better than other forms of writing because they are the least risky, in ratio of writing time to sales. The comparisons are made to provide a realistic writing-to-sales perspective for writers new and old so they can knowledgeably pursue the field best suited to meeting their writing goals, whether those goals are to make money, get in print, display a peculiar creativity, or share knowledge. It also suggests that writers can mix writing fields for a purpose.

An example: A newcomer in whose breast beats the rhythm of a novel might, while feverishly penning 1,000 words of prose a night, be writing queries, then articles, on weekends, to earn cash from writing, see his words published, and fill his sails with much-needed breezes of confidence. Writing doesn't compartmentalize itself; skills flow from one form to another.

Put in other terms, literary history abounds with examples of writers who survived, even thrived, from other kinds of writing—often for newspapers, or in our case in (A) and (B)—while creating high-risk masterpieces. They wrote vocationally in low-risk areas to feed their high-risk writing habits, until they caught on in (C) through (G) to the point where their new field also became low-risk.

If you want to sell 75% of your freelance writing and haven't established a track record in the high-risk areas, then focus on (A) and supplement it with (B) while, if you wish, you write in (C) through (G) in your spare time.

LOW-RISK FORMS OF WRITING

Why are (A) and (B) low-risk forms of writing? Because in (A) you do not write copy until you have better than a 50% chance that it will be bought. And in (B), while you do write the manuscript first, you will send out many copies of that manuscript at the same time. Your chances that more than one, or even a half-dozen, copies of the same article will be bought justify the time spent in its research and preparation.

What you sell in the professional writing world is time, not writing skill. Every writer in print in paying publications must provide copy at a certain level of competence. If not, the copy won't be bought. Once you've reached that skill plateau, you're on equal footing with other professionals. Then you are selling time use, or how much salable material you can produce in a given amount of time.

In the high-risk areas, short stories let's say, your time is poorly spent if you plan to eat from your writing earnings. You must write the entire story and send it blindly to one editor, then another, then a third, and so on, until one (if any) agrees to use it. You can circulate only one manuscript at a time and you have no notion whether an editor will seriously consider it. The wisest short story writer would grind out hundreds and send them out the minute they were finished, each to one editor at a time, hoping by sheer volume to appear in print often enough to scrape out a steady financial return.

That's risky business—high-risk in our terms. Mind

you, we assume the quality of the writing. If it isn't at publication level, the risk is far greater! We're talking about time. If a writer sold one short story in five, and it took him 8 hours to complete each story, that is a 40-hour investment. Let's say he is paid $250 for the story—on publication!

The same writer queries a magazine about a nonfiction article. He sends out three queries before an editor says "Yes, let me see it." He writes the article and it is bought. He has invested 14 hours total, earning $350, paid on acceptance.

The $350 is about what a professional would expect to receive, assuming markets in the middle range. The short story paid $6.25 an hour, after much mailing. To circulate the story five times may have taken six months to a year; the writer may not be paid for another six months to a year, since he must wait until the item is used. His chances of selling the short story again are poor, unless it's in his own anthology.

The article paid $25 an hour, which the writer received when the piece was accepted (or within 30 days of the approval). Even if the editor did not accept the article after asking to see it, which is rare, the writer could still query others and sell it, as is or modified, elsewhere. And the chances of reselling or rewriting the piece and the research are excellent, turning a $25/hour first sale into a $60/hour or $100/hour rewrite or reprint!

Accept for now, then, that there are two categories: low- and high-risk. We will focus in this book only on the one that will bring you a paycheck three out of every four times you write a manuscript.

THE FORMULA

"Amateurs write, then try to sell. Professionals sell, then write."

That is a beacon that will guide you to steady sales and in-print success, though it's not 100% true.

Let's state it another way that irons out the flaws if your goal is to sell 75% of your freelance writing:

> *Write only when you have better than a 50% chance of a sale. Once you've sold a piece, you can increase your profits by selling reprints and rewrites of the same material.*
>
> *You have better than a 50% chance of a sale when you (1) query, and write once you have a positive response to your query, or (2) write to markets where you can simultaneously submit the same material.*

If there's such a thing as a formula to reach the 75% goal, that is it.

A definition of some of the terms will help you better understand how and why the formula works. *Reprints* occur when you sell an article (unchanged or with slight modifications) to other publications after it has appeared in the first publication of sale. *Rewrites* are different articles based on the research and material gathered for the original manuscript.

Please reread the formula and see how it differs from what most novices do. They write something and mail it. If they've not savvy, they send it to the first magazine they encounter. If they're a bit more sophisticated, they ask themselves who would want to read about that topic, then send it to a magazine using that kind of material. The most sophisticated turn to the current *Writer's Market*, make a list of the most likely buyers, and then submit their copy.

Their biggest fault, however, isn't their random market choices. It's that they are writing and sending in the copy cold.

Only beginners submit unsolicited manuscripts to

markets that accept queries. Only beginners spend their time doing all the research and all the writing without having both a publication in mind and a positive reply to a query from an editor of that publication in hand. Only novices sell words without regard to time.

Think about it. If you were the editor and had a choice between two kinds of mail, unsolicited manuscripts (written by beginners) and query letters (written by professionals), which would you read with greater interest? You'd read the query letters first and most seriously, and the unsoliciteds later, if at all.

In one hand you have a manuscript that was sent unsolicited. It's written generally about a subject that may be of interest to your readers. (The beginner wrote it broad enough so that if you rejected it, the same article could be sent to another editor, and so on. . . .)

In your other hand you have a letter written to you about the same topic asking whether you'd like to see a manuscript tailor-made to your readers' interests. The letter is brief and businesslike, yet full of pertinent facts and a sharp quote. It shows writing skill and awareness of your needs. Further, it offers the manuscript in three weeks for your consideration, without obligation. Which will you buy?

If one could simply apply the formula without further explanations, our book would end here. But nothing so promising is ever that simple. So let's consider six factors that further explain how you can sell 75% of your freelance writing while they define the process:

1. the form of writing you pursue
2. your understanding of the marketing process
3. your topic selection

4. your choice of markets
5. the quality of your query letter
6. the form and content of your manuscript copy

Sometimes a seventh element, the availability and quality of illustrations (usually photographic), is also a factor. Except in travel writing, where photos are a definite advantage, illustrations are usually secondary to selling the copy. Therefore a discussion of them will be left to other texts, by illustration specialists.

Let's look a bit more closely at our two low-risk writing fields before we investigate the six factors vital to putting our ideas in print.

QUESTIONS, ANSWERS, AND ADDITIONAL THOUGHTS

Q: When/how is copy submitted?

	Queried?	To whom?	Path followed in "Mechanics"[1]
Nonfiction queried submission	yes	editor	A
Nonfiction simultaneous submission	rarely[2]	(editor)	A/B[2]
Greeting cards	no	—	B
Scripts	yes	agent	A/modified[3]
Fiction	no	—	B
Poetry	no	—	B

[1]See Figure 2, "The Mechanics of Getting Into Print," p. 18.
[2]Some publications require querying, but manuscripts can be sent to others during the querying process.
[3]Substitute the agent in place of the editor you initially contact on path A. The agent will submit the final script to the buyer, instead of the editor.

You don't query fiction. The editors have to read your prose to see whether you've created copy worth buying. Short stories should be sent to the fiction editor in final form, with an SASE (self-addressed stamped envelope).

With novels, first check the library and bookstore to see which publishers offer similar books—it is futile to try to sell your gothic or science fiction masterpiece to a company publishing medical textbooks, for example. List those publishers by number of similar titles and closeness to your subject. Rank your list by purchase probability and preference. Then review the "book publishers" section in the current *Writer's Market* to see how the publishers on your list want to be approached. Finally, one at a time, do what each entry suggests: Send the whole manuscript, representative chapters, etc.

Q: Can I sell fillers?

A: Fillers are just that: They fill odd holes when the editor is pasting up a publication for print. Some remind the reader to renew his subscription, some implore him to support a particular charitable cause, and some are copy bought from freelancers, but the pay is almost always low and slow.

Fillers are generally 1,000 words or less. Some are only a few words long. Prepare yours in regular manuscript fashion and write "FILLER" under the word count. They are unqueried single submissions; no cover letter is required. The editor will either reject them, and you can try to sell them elsewhere, or tell you that the filler is being held and you will be paid when it is used. Sometimes fillers are returned months or years later with the cruelest words known to the freelancer: "Great piece of work. Just wish we could have used it. Good luck in placing it else-where."

Fillers cover the whole spectrum of subjects and writing styles. Often bought are short humor, advice, personality pieces, oddities, anecdotal or ironical insights, jokes, people in history, nostalgia, quips, wordplay, puns, or lists ("Eight Ways to Enjoy Patagonia in the Summer!").

Writer's Market lists thousands of markets for fillers. Don't be deceived by the abundance and by the fact that *Reader's Digest* pays $300+ for humor briefs. In the main this is a nickel-and-dime market. Focus on nonfiction queried submissions for your major sales. Save the scraps from your research and the short inspirational flashes for fillers, then write them, mail them, and get on to something else more lucrative. Unless you're the next Richard Armour or Ogden Nash.

BIBLIOGRAPHY

Boggess, Louise. *How to Write Short Stories That Sell.* Harper & Row, 1984.

Burgett, Gordon. *Empire-Building by Writing and Speaking.* Communication Unlimited, 1988.

Burgett, Gordon. *Self-Publishing to Tightly-Targeted Markets.* Communication Unlimited, 1989.

Duncan, Louise. *How to Write and Sell Your Personal Experiences.* Writer's Digest Books, 1986.

Emerson, Connie. *How to Make Money Writing Fillers.* Writer's Digest Books, 1985.

Engh, Rohn. *Sell and Re-Sell Your Photos,* 2nd ed. Writer's Digest Books, 1987.

Falk, Kathryn. *How to Write a Romance and Get It Published.* NAL, 1984.

Frey, James N. *How to Write a Damn Good Novel*. St Martin's Press, 1987.

Hensley, Dennis E., and Rose Adkins. *Writing for Religious and Other Specialty Markets*. Broadman, 1987.

Ross, Tom and Marilyn. *How to Make Big Profits Publishing City and Regional Books*. Communication Creativity, 1987.

Sandman, Larry, ed. *A Guide to Greeting Card Writing*. Writer's Digest Books, 1984.

Shulman, Joel J. *How to Get Published in Business/Professional Journals*. AMACOM, 1980.

Wilbur, Perry. *How to Write Books That Sell*. Wiley and Sons, 1987.

———■———

He who does not expect a million readers should not write a line.

Goethe, 1749-1832

CHAPTER 2

The Process

There's no magic to marketing, then writing, articles or nonfiction books that sell. The process is shockingly straightforward.

The marketing starts long before the sale and determines what you write and how. It starts with an idea and ends with many sales. This book, in particular this section, explains that process. The only mystery is why others haven't explained it years ago.

There are two complementary guides to the process that could quickly elevate your sales to the 75% plateau—if you find good ideas that others want to read about, follow the guides, and write to the level of the publications in which you want to appear.

"The Mechanics of Getting Into Print," Figure 2 on the next page, graphically shows the path from the idea to sale, resale, and reprint. We will discuss it briefly before integrating the second guide, "How to Prepare and Market Articles That Sell," Figure 3 (p. 24), which breaks the process into 15 steps, with variations for direct submissions.

Figure 2 The Mechanics of Getting Into Print

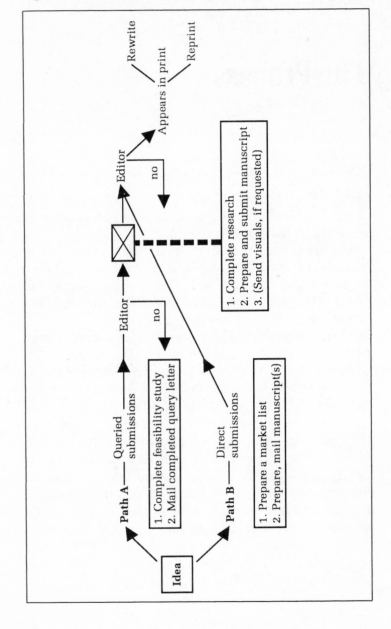

Key to Figure 2

> **Path A** is for most nonfiction articles and books; includes humorous (where humor is the style rather than purpose).
> **Path B** is for simultaneous submissions as well as fiction, fillers, and humor (where humor is the purpose). See Figure 3, "How to Prepare and Market Articles That Sell," p. 24.

TWO PATHS

"The Mechanics of Getting Into Print" follows two paths, (A) for queried submissions and (B) for direct submissions. Both begin with an idea; both end with a sale or a rejection. The differences between the paths are considerable, though they ultimately share the same moment of truth, when the editor reads the manuscript and says yes or no.

The most important difference is when the editor passes first judgment on the idea. On the queried path that judgment is made *before* you expend major time on travel, research, and final composition. With direct submissions, the idea is judged only once: *after* the manuscript is totally researched and written.

Path A: Queried Submissions

On the queried path, you write a letter to an editor asking whether he would consider an article or book about a particular topic written by you. If the editor says no, you write another query to another editor, until one says yes or you run out of editors.

When an editor says yes to a query, indicating that the manuscript will be seriously considered, you complete the research and write the piece, sending it to that editor. You can follow that route along the top of the chart in Figure 2.

What kinds of writing are marketed this way? Non-fiction articles and books, including humorous (where humor is the style rather than the purpose).

Path B: Direct Submissions

The direct submission path, (B), is far simpler to follow but, in the long run, costlier in time and risk. Here you determine the readership, prepare a market list, research the idea, write the manuscript, and send it directly to the editor. What kinds of writing are sold by direct submission? Fiction (short stories and novels), fillers, greeting cards, humor (where humor is the purpose), most newspaper submissions, and some regional, in-flight, and religious material, as indicated in the current *Writer's Market* or by studying the publication.

Simultaneous submissions also follow path (B) and differ from other direct submissions in that many copies of the same item can be sent to different editors simultaneously, as will be explained more fully later in this chapter.

How They Differ

Both paths can lead to the pinnacle—or at least to Fort Knox. One is cautious, with stops and starts, but with greater financial reward. The other is as direct as can be.

Unfortunately for your coffers, the queried and direct submission paths aren't equal when editors make a buying decision. The slower route in time, (A), is far more lucrative than the express lane, (B).

When the editor receives a manuscript on path (A),

he knows it is coming because of the query. Furthermore, by telling you to prepare and submit that article, the editor has a share in its creation, a psychological investment in seeing it succeed. That hook operates in your favor, *if* the final copy lives up to its queried promise. Direct submissions, on the other hand, arrive unexpectedly and must win favor solely on their first-impression merits.

Combine the uncertainty of the directly submitted material's reception with the time invested in its full preparation and you can see why queried submissions are preferable. The latter are never completed until the writer has solid assurance that the finished product will be given full consideration for acceptance and is worth its cost in time and expense.

The only way direct submissions can approach that logic is when many copies of the same manuscript can be sent to different markets at once, on the premise that of, say, a dozen markets, more than one will buy the piece and offset the greater risk its preparation entails.

Let's look at the specifics of both queried and simultaneous submissions, of paths (A) and (B), to set the base for the rest of the book—and, more important, for the rest of your selling/writing future.

THE QUERIED ROUTE

Articles

If every go-ahead resulted in a sale, you would literally sell 100% of what you wrote. Alas, that never happens. My own results and those of my freelancing friends, earlier in our careers and now, indicate that you should easily sell more than half of your go-aheads from the outset, if you provide what you promised in the query and write to the publication's level, and that sales rate will approach 80%–90% as your output increases and an informal client relation-ship develops with editors of publications central to your writing interests.

But that's still not 75% the moment you put this process into practice. Reprints should more than make up the difference. That is, by selling "second rights" to articles, with little or no copy change, after they have been in print in the targeted publication, you can quickly boost your average to 100% or more. An example: You sell a general-interest item to a mag-azine, first rights, for $350. It appears in print and you offer it to five others, as a reprint. Two buy it. If your original sale was from the first go-ahead, you sold 300% of what you wrote! Even if it was from the sec-ond go-ahead, and you did some rewriting of the text for the second market, you wrote it twice and sold it three times, or 150%! (See Chapter 10, "Reselling the Sales," for details.)

The key, though, is not the reprints or subsequent sales, as nice as they are and as much as they should be sought. It's that you don't invest time and cost in an article until you have the relative assurance of the initial go-ahead.

Books

Nonfiction book sales are harder to calculate, since reprints are unlikely. On the other hand, a second-step bailout is usually involved. You query in a simi-lar fashion, then research and write only when you receive a go-ahead. The positive response often indi-cates that a contract will be issued upon receipt and approval of a certain number of chapters, usually two or three. So you must write, fully and with total dedication, that much copy before you get a financial commitment from the publisher.

The ratio becomes twisted at that point. Few book editors encourage writers unless the editors are serious about following through, so the go-ahead in itself probably approaches a 75% potential selling ratio. If the writer clears that crucial first hurdle—if the sample chapters are accepted—the contract is usually drawn up and honored. But the deal can collapse later, if the writer fails to produce the book, the quality of subsequent chapters is inferior to that of the samples, the publishing house folds, etc. The length of the time needed to write a book, plus human and business vagaries, fill book writing/selling with far more potential pitfalls than articles. Still, most professionals consider this a safer path for fiscal follow-through than articles, mainly because of the contract and the amount of money involved. So while percentage is harder to prove, the path is firmer.

A Plan of Attack

The question, then, is how do we write these literary Geiger counters so we can quickly strike pay dirt?

Phrased like a novice. The professional would ask, "How do we sell, then write?" For articles and nonfiction books, the process is almost the same.

Figure 2 suggests the key elements in their proper order:

1. idea
2. query
3. go-ahead
4. research

5. writing
6. mailing
7. check cashing
8. rewriting and/or reprinting

"How to Prepare and Market Articles That Sell," Figure 3, outlines the steps for taking an idea and turning it into profitable print. The process varies so little for articles and nonfiction books that the same guide, with a few obvious word changes, applies to both.

Figure 3 How to Prepare and Market Articles That Sell

1. In one sentence, what is the subject of the article you want to write and sell?
2, Who would benefit from reading your article? Who would be most interested? What kinds of readers would select your specific subject from a variety of choices? Rank all those potential readers in order, placing those who would derive the most benefits first.
3. Which publications do these readers buy and read? Prepare a market list of those publications that are the most likely to buy your manuscript.
4. In addition to the publications checked in (3), it is necessary to review the broader publishing field for articles similar or identical to yours. Therefore, you must check both the *Reader's Guide to Periodical Literature* and specific subject indexes for at least the previous three years, then
   a. list the articles that are closest to your subject, in order with the most similar first: subject, author, title, publication, page reference, length, and when they appeared. Where the subjects appear to be very similar, how does yours differ?
   b. cross-check newspaper indexes for the past three years and provide the same information.
5. Have the publications listed in (3) and (4) printed arti-

cles within the past three years that are similar to the
one you propose?

6. After each publication, note the name of the person you
   should contact (editor, managing editor, etc.), with title
   and address. Then provide the following information
   about each publication:

   a. Does it pay on acceptance or publication?
   b. How much does it pay for articles as long as yours?
   c. Does it prefer a query or a direct submission?
   d. How often is it published?
   e. What percentage of it is written by freelancers?
   f. What is its preferred manuscript length?
   g. Is any other information provided that will affect
      its placement on your list?

7. Now rank your market list in priority order, based on
   when the buyers pay (on acceptance or on publication),
   how much, the frequency of publication, and the percentage of freelance material used per issue.

8. Read the latest issues of your target publication, front to
   back. Select the articles that are the most similar, in
   form if not topic, to the piece you will prepare. Outline
   each article. Write out the lead and conclusion of each,
   by hand. Follow the 12 steps in Figure 5, "How to
   Study a Printed Magazine Article," p. 76. Attempt to
   identify the publication's readers by age, sex, occupa-
   tion, income range, education, residence, and other
   pertinent factors.

9. To verify the availability of resource information

   a. read as many of the articles in (5) as necessary or
      possible, then list the sources of information found
      in each,
   b. consult the card catalog and list books you will re-
      fer to for factual information: title, author, call
      number, date of publication, and library, and
   c. list the people you should consult for additional
      information and quotes, working with the refer-
      ence librarian for information that you do not al-
      ready have: their name, position, and current affili-
      ation (if related to the topic), academic title and de-

grees (if relevant), and reasons for their being consulted.

10. From the information you've gathered on the specific target publication and the research you've done on your topic, select the material needed to write a professional query letter. Verify its accuracy.

11. Write a selling query letter to an editor of your target publication. If you do not receive a positive reply, write a query letter to the editor of the next publication on your list, and so on, one editor at a time, until an editor does respond positively. Repeat as much of (9) as necessary for each new publication queried.

12. When you receive that positive response to your query, plan your article to determine what is still needed to finish it.

13. Complete the needed research.

14. Write the manuscript in final draft form. Include, on separate paper, at least five additional, different leads.

15. Select the best lead, edit the draft, type a final manuscript (keeping a copy), and mail it, with illustrations (if needed and available), to the editor who gave you the go-ahead.

Variations for simultaneous submissions:

When you prepare your market list, review it to avoid circulation overlap. Then, rather than following the querying process, prepare a basic manuscript, avoiding specific references (usually geographic or temporal) that would prevent universal or long-term use of your material. Make copies of the basic manuscript. Where it would enhance the manuscript's salability, add a personalized cover note or letter. Mail the submissions to the respective editors.

Of the 15 steps, the first 10 precede writing the query letter, the 11th step describes that critical action, and the 4 that follow talk about actual manuscript preparation. As you become familiar with the guide and the research and selling tools used in the early steps, however, the time spent will come close to reversing the 11:4 (pre- to post-query) ratio, and the wisdom of having many queries in circulation will become as obvious as the process is easy to do.

You will also see how important it is to find an idea that is salable, then mate it to the people who would pay to read about it. In other words, tightly match the idea to an identifiable readership, whether you start with the idea or the reader.

You may be surprised to see how much emphasis is placed on writing like others, at least while you develop your writing skill, and how uniqueness and forging new styles and paths are discouraged, at least initially, if you wish to sell often and well. That may appear to be a painful compromise between art and exigency—in fact, it probably is when you are new to the field—but the consistent excellence and originality seen in nonfiction, within widely accepted bounds, indicate somewhat the reverse, that considerable room for expression exists for those who learn to wield deftly the tools of their craft, words, within the accepted stylistic limits.

Last, the 15 steps are not carved in marble. On occasion they may work better in a slightly different order. Some may be omitted entirely once you have become familiar with the process and the elements necessary to sell, then write. With practice you will learn how to mold them to fit your fashion. But for beginners without proven substitutes of their own, the steps are altered or omitted at peril.

Because nonfiction simultaneous submissions are a deviation from the process just outlined, the next section will deal with them and the final segment of "How to Prepare and Market Articles That Sell" more fully.

THE SIMULTANEOUS SUBMISSION ROUTE

Nonfiction simultaneous submissions is the second area where selling 75% of one's writing both regularly and quickly is highly likely.

The process is simple too. You get an idea, research it, prepare a market list, write the manuscript, reproduce as many copies of that manuscript as you have primary markets, send a manuscript to each with a cover note and an SASE, and wait to cash the checks!

Alas, it's not quite that slick and gilded. For one thing, you must do all the research and writing without any indication of a sale. You might ship off a dozen copies of the same masterpiece to as many hungry markets, only to have them all rejected. It happens to even the most gifted professionals. So your selling percentage would be zero while your time expenditure, plus preparation costs and postage, could be considerable.

Even worse, when you do sell, most simultaneous markets pay poorly, or at least well below their queried counterparts. If you make half as much per sale by the (B) route, you need twice as many sales to stay even. And they are written at 100% risk.

Yet your numbers can be spectacular. You write "the" article about visiting the regal palaces in Haiti, Mexico, and Brazil and zip it off to 18 newspaper travel editors. Six find it irresistible—4 buy the piece with black and white photos, 2 want just the prose. Since you sold exactly the same article six times, you sold at a 600% ratio. And you earned about $1,000 total. Who can argue with that kind of success? Except that you could have earned roughly the same with two similar sales, with photos, to middle-level travel magazines—or to just one at a higher pay range. And since you would have queried the magazines and received a go-ahead first, the risk would have been far less!

(As you will see in later chapters, you can also do both: sell manuscripts to queried and simultaneous submission markets about the same general topic at the same time, reducing the risk even more while increasing your income potential. The articles must be significantly different, however.)

What makes simultaneous submissions worth doing is the possibility that more than one market will buy the same material. Since you can send the very same copy to 4 or 10 or 25 publications simultaneously, at some point the potential of multiple sales overrules the element of risk, aided of course by the choice of your topic and your writing skill.

Where can you simultaneously submit nonfiction copy? To newspaper travel sections and weekly supplements, as well as religious, regional, and in-flight magazines.

Newspaper Travel

Travel writing may be the easiest type of writing to sell. Almost any publication uses either travel or factual information with a unique geographic setting, and the American appetite for movement and information about other lands and people grows daily. Best yet, if well receipted and justified, most or all of the expenses for trips can be deducted from your taxes.

With the exception of the *Wall Street Journal, Christian Science Monitor, New York Times,* and *USA Today,* or other national newspapers, you can simultaneously send the same manuscript, unqeuried, to newspaper travel sections in cities where papers don't overlap in circulation or distribution. (For most, primary circulation doesn't extend beyond 100 miles.)

Where they do overlap, using Chicago as an example, you might send it to the *Tribune* first; if rejected, to the *Sun-Times* next, and, if still rejected, to the Milwaukee and South Bend, Indiana, papers, which are too close to Chicago to buy simultaneously what appears in the dominant metropolitan daily. Continue down your list of separate circulation spheres until the potential buyers say yes or you run out of newspapers!

The pay for newspaper travel is generally low: $85–$150 per article bought, plus $10–$25 per black and white photo used. Color slides are rarely purchased from freelancers. If one paper is interested in the manuscript, three or four usually are, with about half those buying from one to four photos. That can bring you $500+ total for a fairly short piece.

At the outset don't compete against the travel editors by sending full-length articles several thousand words long. The editor usually writes the main piece—or buys it from another travel editor. Given a choice between his own article, another editor's, or yours, guess who loses? Shoot for one of the many "second" articles regularly bought from freelancers. Keep yours in the 1,000-to-1,600-word range, preferably about 1,250, at least until your name is well known and your writing respected.

An excellent book about travel writing is Louise Purwin Zobel's *The Travel Writer's Handbook* (Writer's Digest Books, 1985). It contains an extra gem that idea seekers will particularly treasure. Buried in the appendix on page 251 is a section called "The Twelve Most Popular Types of Travel Articles."

Apart from its obvious value to travel writers, this section shows a dozen ways to see ideas in general. It shows the kind of mental flexibility a writer needs to find precisely the right approach or angle to match an idea to a readership or a market.

Zobel's book may be the best available about the researching and writing process in general. It is highly recommended for all writers. For the idealess, a useful report called "300 Ideas for Travel Articles" is available from Communication Unlimited, P.O. Box 6405, Santa Maria, CA 93456.

Newspaper Weekly Supplements

Submitting to newspaper weekly supplements follows the same rule, except for length: Send only to those where circulation or distribution don't overlap. So if you wish to sell to *Parade, Family Weekly,* or a similar national supplement, try them one at a time first. If there are no takers, you can submit the article simultaneously to the regional newspapers. Some are listed in *Writer's Market* under "Regional Publications."

Here you confront a dilemma that will also be present in religious, regional, and in-flight markets. Some weekly supplement editors want to be queried, while others will accept direct submissions. Since you are writing the manuscript first, counting on the sheer number distributed to produce enough sales to offset the time spent on research and writing, what do you do?

If the piece is pure humor, forget the query and send it to all possible markets. But if it's humorous or straight and thus queriable if sent singly, (1) send copies to all possible simultaneous markets, and (2) send a query, individually written to each editor, to those markets that want query letters.

Make sure that the query describes precisely what

you've written, in the same style and tone. Don't mention that the actual copy has already been penned. On the other hand, indicate that it will be offered to other newspaper weekly supplements outside the editor's circulation area (or to religious publications of other faiths or sects, regionals in other parts of the country, or in-flights covering other parts of the nation, if your primary market is in one of those fields).

Should a queried editor want to see the piece, send him a copy of the simultaneous submission. If he wants it written in a special way or to a different length, or suggests some other literary revision, alter the basic copy to meet the editor's demands and send it. That way you get the best of both worlds, querying and simultaneous submission.

Most newspaper supplements want local items, or at least something their readers can immediately relate to. Local items are difficult if the piece is to be sold simultaneously nationwide. So focus on topics of immediate interest everywhere. Humor or humorous items work well, particularly about something everybody has experienced or will: the blind date, cooking your first Thanksgiving turkey, that 10-year reunion—to pick three evergreens. Holiday topics, investigative reporting in the consumer affairs area, medical discoveries, nostalgia about famous people or major events are other items you can sell from coast to coast.

What else do newspapers buy? The best way to find out what they might buy from you is to read their pages and see who wrote the pieces. In addition to travel, weekly supplement, and op-ed pieces, which are the items most often purchased from outsiders, check to see whether the newspaper uses an occasional offbeat feature, food, or business article by a freelancer. Often the byline will say "special for" that publication.

Out-of-town newspapers can often be found in the library's periodicals section. Call or write local papers and ask the specific editor whether he buys freelance copy. (But don't call the weekly supplements or any other magazines.) And check the *Writer's Market* "regional" entry.

To find the editors of the respective sections of the newspapers, check *The Working Press of the Nation* or other guides your reference librarian suggests. As a rule of thumb, the larger and more independent the newspaper, the more likely it is to buy freelance material. Payment also tends to be related to size, though newspapers in general pay less, often far less, than magazines.

Submitting Photography Simultaneously to Newspapers

While I dwell very little on photography in this book, deferring to others more experienced, there is one marketing technique I have used over the years when submitting photography simultaneously to newspapers that isn't well covered elsewhere.

Rather than querying, with simultaneous submissions to newspapers the first contact is the actual article itself, plus a cover note attached to the front page (see Figure 10, p. 121). In that note you indicate the kind and quantity of photos you have available. In the example I offered 36 black and whites (b/w's)—or I would pick the five best.

Note that I offer b/w's. Newspapers almost never buy slides from untried freelancers, so your sales will be 95% or more black and white. If you have slides, offer them too, of course. But always take b/w's if your market is newspaper travel. (Making b/w's from color slides can be done, but it is a bit expensive and some of the sharpness is lost.)

If the editor wants to see my b/w's, he lets me know via the SASE. In the meantime I have my film developed as proof or contact sheets, not prints. (These are contact sheets 8 x 10" or larger on which the negative strips have been laid and developed, producing 20 or 36 small prints about an inch square. Contact sheets cost considerably less than prints.)

So when the editor asks to see the 36 samples, I select the best 36 from the 100 or so shots I usually take. I cut these small prints from the contact sheets and affix them to several sheets of typing-size paper, with a number under each. Then I type a caption page, giving a one-line explanation of each print, identifying each by the number. I put my name and address on every sheet of paper and send them to the editor with a large SASE for their return.

The editor usually selects from three to eight prints, circling them or giving me their numbers, and I separate and send those negatives in the next mail, wrapping each negative carefully to avoid scratching. I also send a more complete caption for each of the prints chosen. (If the editor told me to pick the best five, I would skip the previous step and send five small prints, the five negatives, and captions for each.)

At this point the editor makes 8 x 10 prints from my negatives, uses what he needs, returns the negatives—and often the giant prints! My costs are modest, I've yet to lose a negative in the mail, and since editors request photos at different times, the 100 shots cover all needs. One caution, though. If the photos are once-in-a-lifetime shots, or valuable to you, have a second set of negatives made and keep those in a safe place!

How do the shots stretch so far? If you have 100 to start with and send 36 to each editor, with a bit of pinching on the third you can send three sets out at a time. If the editor uses 8 maximum, the minute the rejects come back they can be sent to another editor. It works. Been doing it for years and I've sold plenty of b/w's. But if you think it will be too few, just offer 16 shots instead of 36 and your negatives will go twice as far.

Religious Publications

Often you can sell the same manuscript simultaneously to religious publications. If you could find a topic of equal interest to, say, the Baptists, Coptics, Catholics, and Druids—God knows what it would be—you could send it to one publication per group, noting "Baptist [or whatever] edition" in the upper right hand corner of the first page under the word count. But if there are three Druid publications, for example, you must send it to one at a time. Many religious publications want to be queried, even though they accept simultaneous submissions, so the process explained for weekly supplements would apply.

Writing for juvenile religious magazines can be a particularly good place to start if you need credits to prove to yourself that you can write professionally. Why? Because the pay scale is so low there is little competition—which doesn't mean your writing doesn't have to be good and fit their needs. But it does mean you can sell more easily. The article needn't be goody-goody, either, or mention God every third word. Ask for complimentary copies, study them, and give them one better.

Regional Publications

Regional publications follow an identical process. An article that would interest readers in Seattle, Los Angeles, Kentucky, Miami, and Maine could either be sent simultaneously or queried, or both, since the primary readership of each is far from the other. You can even mix newspaper travel sections, regionals, and in-flights as targets for simultaneous submissions as long as they don't overlap.

In-flight Magazines

Articles for in-flights, as you have guessed, are also marketed the same way. You can't sell your article to a national or international airline and expect to sell to any or at least many other in-flights, since overlap is once more the bane. Alaska Airlines, Mexicana, and Air New Zealand don't overlap; two small airlines in the same state would. A map or a call to a travel agency will give you some idea, and a look at the "in-flight" section in *Writer's Market* will also help.

QUESTIONS, ANSWERS, AND ADDITIONAL THOUGHTS

Don't be a dummy like I was.

When I began writing it took me a year to learn about *Writer's Market*, and another six months to read the first 30 or 40 pages, which gave the general guidelines that freelancers should know. Then I ignored the querying process for probably three more years. It sounded too slow and too much like the kind of thing that somebody writing for the *New Yorker* would do, which was as far from my rural Illinois dreams as sunbathing in Alaska.

Instead, I improvised and "did it my way" and sold so little I used the word "writer" with caution around my family and friends lest I be blown away by their gales of laughter. Eventually I tried querying, it worked, and I built my own order around it. Soon enough I was selling more than 100%, that continued for years, I started sharing the process with students and others, and now you have this book.

The point? Don't be a dummy like I was. Don't shy away from proven methods. Query. Study other articles in the magazines where you want to appear. Interview, cull facts, resell, do it all. But do it. And substitute your own system or process only when it proves to be more effective than those already followed by professionals in your writing field.

Finally, write. Every day, write. Set a quota in words or time. Produce copy. Sound obvious? Most "writers" don't write. They talk writing. Or think writing. Or they read about writing. Be different. Sell. Write. And write nonqueried material in between.

Q: Should you write only in your areas of expertise?

A: If you're a nurse, for example, should you write only for nursing publications? Heavens no, but it's an advantage you'd waste by ignoring your expertise. Spending years in a career provides abundant resource knowledge. On the other hand, almost any true article writer can write about almost anything.

Q: What kind of degrees do you need to be a writer?

A: All you need is literacy and a bit of push. A degree won't hurt you, of course. Literacy can come from having one. But you don't need a degree to write.

BIBLIOGRAPHY

American Society of Journalists and Authors. *The Complete Guide to Writing Nonfiction.* Writer's Digest Books, 1983.

Baker, Samm S. *Writing Nonfiction That Sells.* Writer's Digest Books, 1986.

Biagi, Shirley. *How to Write and Sell Magazine Articles.* Prentice-Hall, 1981.

Burgett, Gordon. *Query Letters/Cover Letters: How They Sell Your Writing.* Communication Unlimited, 1986.

Burgett, Gordon. *Ten Sales from One Article Idea.* Communication Unlimited, 1981.

Casewit, Curtis. *Freelance Writing: Advice from the Pros.* Macmillan, 1985.

Cool, Lisa C. *How to Sell Every Magazine Article You Write.* Writer's Digest Books, 1986.

Cool, Lisa C. *How to Write Irresistible Query Letters.* Writer's Digest Books, 1987.

Emerson, Connie. *Write on Target: Triple Your Magazine Sales Through Market Analysis.* Writer's Digest Books, 1981.

Fredette, Jean M. *Writer's Digest Handbook of Magazine Article Writing.* Writer's Digest Books, 1988.

Gunther, Max. *Writing the Modern Magazine Article.* The Writer, 1986.

Kevles, Barbara. *Basic Magazine Writing.* Writer's Digest Books, 1986.

Meredith, Scott. *Writing to Sell.* Harper & Row, 1987.

Newcomb, Duane. *How to Sell and Re-Sell Your Writing.* Writer's Digest Books, 1987.

Young, Jordan. *How to Become a Successful Freelance Writer.* Moonstone Press, 1983.

———————■———————

No man but a blockhead ever wrote except for money.

Samuel Johnson, 1709-84

PART TWO

The Steps

CHAPTER 3

Picking and
Defining a Topic

STARTING WITH AN IDEA

Ideas per se aren't the most important element of getting into print. Almost any idea well enough written and marketed with sufficient tenacity could find a lodging on some page—if you don't care where, how much you receive for your labors, or how long placing it takes. After all, given enough funds and common sense you could always self-publish!

But our intent here is to get you into print often and profitably, so we must seek ideas that are easily and widely marketed. That's not hard to do. Remember that people want to read about themselves, as they are or were or might be, in fact or fantasy. Then write accordingly.

The easiest way to find ideas that sell is to find out what readers care enough about to buy.

Cashing In on the Quotidian

What stops most new writers in search of a salable topic is their limited experience. "I've never done anything that others want to read about," they say. Like climbing Everest or swimming the Indian Ocean or winning the Nobel Prize.

So what? Somebody did climb Everest, and the Nobel Prizes are won annually. Write about those people. Few who attain high positions or do unusual things write about them. That's for you.

Yet most articles aren't about extraordinary deeds or people. They are about everyday topics, mainly about meeting basic physical and emotional needs.

For years I divided my writing classes into four groups, each with the task of analyzing the contents of current magazines in the general, men's, women's, and specialty (usually running or travel) categories. They were to place the articles and columns in one of two categories: "everyday" or "other."

"Everyday" included the kinds of concerns that most people share at any time, about jobs, school, cars, security, health, income, dreams, playtime, children, death, sex, happiness, cooking, sports, gardening, appearance, dress. . . .

"Other" items tended to be unique, exotic, bizarre —including singular, once-in-a-lifetime achievements or experiences. This category included articles about UFO visitors, gold hunts on the Amazon River, winning the Irish Sweepstakes. . . .

With boring regularity, the "everyday" items made up about 80% of the total in all four classifications. Even in the specialty publications the ratio held. In the running magazines, for example, while the slant was to runners, the topics were still about the runners' physical and emotional needs: diet, shoes, complexion, heart attacks, running as an antidepressant, etc.

The best topics for selling articles touch one's ordinary existence. People want to read about themselves, as they are, were, or want to be. Stick close to these themes; let the reader see himself in your prose.

Don't write about your spouse who snores. Write about snoring spouses, with enough examples—famous and familiar—that the reader will shout huzzahs at being spared or will nod, tiredly, at every word in instant recognition.

Don't talk about divorce in Bali; write about "How to Mend Your Marital Fence." Don't write about Freud and dreams; tell how your readers' dreams can be paths to a better tomorrow.

Use frequency of thought as a gauge. If you think of the same thing every week, write about it—you probably have a moneymaker. If you think of something every day, you have a gold mine! Get it in print! (But if you think of it five times a day, you may have an obsession!)

Articles about child care regularly appear in popular commercial magazines, for example. Why? Because almost every reader cares for children, did, or will. As long as there are children to care for, it will be a topic to be written about. Find new ways to write about child care and they will be printed. Explain the new ways that others are doing old things, some old ways by which they do new things, and new ways to do new things, and you will have sales.

The newcomers' lament that they've never done anything or "there's nothing to write about" rings hollow. Since life is the starting point, simply find elements of everyday living that interest others, then research and write about them.

How can newlyweds afford homes today? What inoculations are no longer required—and why? How did your neighbor, and scores like her, hold down a job and raise a family while earning her B.A.? Are there any motion sickness cures on the horizon? Do the motion-activated burglary alarms really work? Is the 12-month school about to become a reality nationwide? Can you learn Basque by tape while you sleep? Those are the stories you sell.

You needn't know much about any of them. Find people who do; seek experts, studies, books, reports. Combine the facts, quotes, and anecdotes and sell the copy. Better yet, use your neighbor as the spark, find others like her in different parts of the country, gather some information about older folks seeking degrees, include numbers and trends, and you have both a local article, with her as the focus, and a national piece, with her and many more examples.

Look around and think. There are more ideas within reach than you could write about in a lifetime.

The third lament that stops novices before they begin: "Everything has been written about!" Which is close to being true: Almost everything worth writing about has been and is being written about. Worse yet, by professionals!

But this is the best news you can hear, because the topics that are attracting those writers are the topics that sell. Beginners run from them; professionals race to them. It's the readers' interest that tells the writer, new or old, what to write about. And common sense that tells you to find a new angle, a new approach, a new study or expert opinion or discovery, then get it on paper and into print.

Some writers make a livelihood from one subject only. Handsome incomes are earned from subjects like cancer, the Kennedys, divorce, baseball, space. You'll see how to get started on a one-subject career when we discuss "topic-spoking" in Chapter 11. Just remember Thomas Edison, who said that the truest lesson he learned was not to invent something that others didn't want. So don't write about subjects that others won't read.

To prosper, do the reverse: Write most about what affects the greatest number of people the deepest. Stick to basics, to topics that touch the heart of human existence.

STARTING WITH A PUBLICATION

There are two ways to match words to readers. The most common, at least for beginners, is to find an idea, then the most appropriate market for it. The second way is to start with a magazine and divine, then meet, its needs.

To do the second, think of its editors as farmers who plant and disseminate ideas to nurture the mind. If you want to sell your ideas to editors, you'd best see what they have been planting the past few years, the kind of ideas they're most familiar with and used to cultivating, then offer some new seeds that will also take root there.

First pick a specialized kind of magazine—travel, auto, religious, animal care—and zero in on the top three serving that readership. Ask your reference librarian whether and where each magazine is indexed. If a magazine isn't, see whether it prints an annual index a certain month each year.

Find the last three—or six or twelve—issues of each magazine and prepare a two-column list for each publication. Separate the lists into (1) articles and (2) departments/columns. Under each, note the subject and the author of every item printed.

See which of the authors listed appear in the magazine's masthead. That will show you the percentage of copy prepared in-house vs. that bought from freelancers. If the magazines are listed in the current *Writer's Market*, that percentage may also be included in the write-up. Double-checking with this list will show any movement toward increasing or decreasing freelance purchases.

Study the list. Topics regularly covered by a department or column aren't likely to be bought as articles. Recent articles show what that readership expects on those pages. Some will show seasonal expectations, others indicate geographic preferences. Does the magazine print humor, history, fillers, controversy? Is it deadly serious or a mixture of lighter pieces plus "think" items? Do the titles indicate the age of the readers or their economic status?

A travel magazine that stresses "seeing the country for $10 a day," "the liveliest hostels for the cyclist," and "how to pack perishables to last from border to border" isn't directed at the jet set or seniors with limited mobility. If you plan to write for those pages, think "low-budget, outdoor, young" seeking practical, detailed how-to advice.

Now compare the lists from all three magazines. How do they differ? Might a subject covered in a column in one be appropriate for an article in another? Mark your observations on each list. If articles about the same topic appeared in two or three magazines, how did the approaches vary? What differences in readership can you deduce?

Where does the index fit in? Study it to get a longer perspective of items used and to note seasonal preferences. If the March issue has traditionally been dedicated to spring cleaning or planting the garden or planning the summer vacation, you know the kinds of ideas best presented for use at that time.

Some topics appear regularly in magazines because they are central to its readers' interests and expectations. Others sit on the fringe, and editors often observe a three-year pause before returning to those interesting but marginal themes. So if you want to write about one of the latter, a look at the indexes of the three top magazines in that field will tell where the subject has not appeared for three years or longer.

A close scrutiny of the rival magazines over the past few years will also show where they are heading and how they have traditionally differed. It will provide topic boundaries beyond which they don't tread. It will suggest accepted ways of treating new ideas— or new ways of presenting old ideas.

Now make a list of 10 or 15 topics or ideas within the subject range of all three magazines, check to see how each magazine has treated the topics, and guess which approaches would most closely match each publication's needs. Let's say they are travel magazines and one caters to the low-budget bargain hunters, a second to the well-heeled eager to see the beauty of nature in comfort, and the third to those seeking adventure, the wilds, and controlled danger.

If you want to write about Ecuador, to the first you might suggest the Indian fairs, one every day of the week in Quito or a short bus trip away. The second might be perfect for the Galapagos voyage. And the third, a canoe expedition up the turbulent Paushi-Yaco and Chapano rivers to pan for gold and see caimans, parrots, anacondas, and flash floods.

That's how to extract ideas and approaches from a magazine study. Find out what editors want by analyzing what they've used. Sound like copycat journalism? So what? Runners will read about running until their arches fall; travelers will court culture shock reading about travel. They buy magazines to satisfy their curiosities or needs. If you want to be paid to appear in print, help satisfy them in new and exciting ways.

IDEA SHORTCUTS

Here are a few that might stir up a salable suggestion:

Holidays

Not very original, yet a built-in preseason headache for editors is how to approach the evergreens in a fresh, exciting way. Almost everything has been tried for Christmas, New Year's, Easter, the Fourth of July, and Thanksgiving—but try again.

One warning: You must query far in advance of the holiday. Some Christmas issues are pasted *a year* in advance, and most are ready to go by June! *Writer's Market* generally advises you about earlier holiday submissions, but take nothing for granted. Even without the advice, six months minimum for most holidays, a year for Christmas/New Year's. Far better that they hold your prose a few weeks than your having to wait another year!

The *historical* approach sometimes yields new fruit: the origin of the celebration, how it was observed back then, ancient practices we still follow, source of the name, and so on. Even if some of the material is gray with age, the editors return to the topic with regularity. Give it a new slant and see it in print.

Universality of the holiday is another angle that delights readers. Where else is Arbor Day celebrated? What do the Portuguese do on Christmas? What are the counterparts to Thanksgiving abroad?

Changing times can be wrapped around holidays.

Greased trolley lines and tipped outhouses no longer signify Halloween, and how does the fragmented family maintain at least a semblance of the family tie during Yuletide? What about a look at the long-distance phone call tallies holiday by holiday? Greeting card numbers up or down?

New gift ideas are always sought by readers, as are new ways of sending, wrapping, and exchanging gifts. New ways to celebrate find families camping on Christmas, rest homes visited on Valentine's, soldiers being invited to homes on Easter.

Anecdotal pieces can tie famous names to holiday events: "Teddy Roosevelt's Christmas Tree," "Daniel Boone's Fourth of July," and 1,000 others. Famous people celebrate events. Tie them to the holidays and the pool is endless.

Dates

Anniversaries are a reason to write about a past event. Or you can focus on a year, a person related to an anniversary, the anniversary of a discovery or invention, a curious juxtaposition (the number of great artists alive in 1900), nostalgia.

Where do you find the dates to build stories around? Ask your reference librarian to see the "date books" in the stacks. They will tell you what happened in Egypt in 1626, England in 1702, or Chicago on May 12, 1926. Or you can find those facts by fields: political news, religious, artistic, social. Want to know what happened on June 17? They can tell you that too.

If the date is within the past 100 or so years, the newspaper indexes will give you a day-by-day account. Writing a centenary piece in 1990 will be simple: Go to the New York Times index, then microfilm,

and see what took place in 1890. Do the same with local papers, and check the *Reader's Guide to Periodical Literature* for more in-depth magazine pieces to
see what folks were thinking and reading.

As with holiday pieces, give your query plenty of
lead time. Six months isn't too long, and at least three
for newspaper weekly supplements, which frequently
use this sort of thing, with a local tie-in.

Leading Questions

These can also set your mind roaming into fertile
fields. The six that work best for me are:

1. What if . . .
2. What about . . .
3. What happened to . . .
4. Why can't . . .
5. What would happen if . . .
6. How did . . .

Complete the leading line and work the answers, or
the questions themselves, into salable copy. For example, "What would happen if we made the minimum college admission age 30?" "What if another
Jesus showed up in America?" "How did Bobbie the
dog find his way home from Indiana to Oregon by a
route he had never seen?"

Leading questions set the mind in motion. A focus
follows, then a query, and a hunt for answers.

Newspapers

You know where to find the best article ideas? In
newspapers, which are by far the best single source of

future articles. But isn't "old news" unsalable? And what about the rights problem?

Forget the "rights problem." There is none. News is facts, which are public domain. Anyway, most newspapers are not copyrighted unless the symbol appears by the item, and that simply covers the writing.

You want to extract the essence of the piece, combine it with other facts, and create your own article. A short item about piranhas dumped into the Jacuzzi at a health spa? You've read about other problems at health spas: damaged Nautilus equipment, peepholes in the women's dressing room wall, goldfish in the bottled water. So you combine these into an article about security at the spas.

There is a natural time progression in print. Today an item appears in the newspaper, a short piece with a fact or two. Tomorrow, more. Over the days the facts add up, change, new names appear, emphasis shifts . . . Newspaper stories are raw and developing.

The same material, in a fuller and more polished form, appears in the magazines next, a few days to a few months later. Somebody plucked that material from the newspapers, reworked and added to it, and wrote the article for the magazine. Just as somebody will write the book that will appear about a year from the first newspaper release, since most books are articles writ long.

The process is simple enough: Extract the part of the newspaper clipping that can be expanded on, widen or tighten the focus, ask the questions that come from the material, identify the readers who will be affected by the answers, query the publication(s) they read, and write when you have a go-ahead. The person performing this journalistic alchemy could be you.

Am I advocating theft? Never! Just borrowing in the

time-honored journalistic tradition. Facts are public domain. If a writer is kind enough to reveal the facts, they are revealed, to be freely re-revealed by you. If you use that writer's words, you must give credit. If you almost use those words, you are perilously close to parallel plagiarism. So do neither, just zero in on already dug ground to find bones for your article. Double-check, of course, where possible. You are responsible for the facts used, whatever their origin.

THE IDEA BOOK

As we have seen, a significant amount of your writing success comes from what you write about. Yet many writers, otherwise well organized, are quite haphazard about keeping track of ideas.

A three-ring holder with 750 pages of paper, one page for each idea, may work best. To fill it would require three ideas a day for five days a week, giving yourself a two-week vacation per annum whenever you choose. A banker's schedule for moneymaking ideas.

Do you need 750 ideas a year for writing success? Hardly. Since you define success in your own terms, the number of ideas is probably less a factor than the number of sales and the income earned. And to earn a good wage you may need only 3 to 5 ideas if you topic-spoke (see Chapter 11). If you develop them one at a time, 20 to 35 ideas may be enough since each idea can generate reprints, rewrites, and other remunerative spinoffs.

Then why should you record 750 ideas a year? Because you can't be certain when you record them which will result in a sale. And because the act of identifying ideas and writing them down on a daily

Figure 4 Pages from an Idea Book

Date: 3/1

Idea: *Backpacking by bike:* to reach the off-the-road campsites, leave cycle, hike in farther without aching legs and back. Are bikes safe if left alone? How can they be protected? Is this done anywhere? Advantages? How can gear be attached to cycle and carried later?

Markets: cycling
backpacking
outdoors/wilderness
sports equipment

Date: 5/19

Idea: *Backpacking by plane:* why couldn't you fly into area, then backpack even farther into bush? Leave plane? dropped off, picked up later? Is this done for backpackers; it is for hunters and fishermen. Could they go on same trip, split costs and separate when they arrive? Could even fly on commercial lines, take bus to bush, hike in. Find examples.

Markets: aviation
in-flight
tour
backpacking/hiking
outdoors/wilderness
regional: Alaska, West, etc.

---

basis may be, in the long run, more valuable than the specific ideas themselves.

Figure 4 shows how a page in the idea book might look.

No research is required for idea book entries. The "Idea" items in Figure 4 are questions you have that you want answered by the article or items you think others want to know about it. The list by "Markets" is a first guess at where you'd look for markets. The entries provide just enough information to explain the idea and get you moving in the right selling direction.

The idea book also provides an ideal place to store subsequent information about ideas that are still in their nascent stages. Let's say that you read a short item in the newspaper about a backpacker doing what you had thought up for Figure 4. Clip the item and tape it to that idea book page. Or you hear of a local outdoorsman who's done the same. Note his name in the idea book in case you write the article later and need an interview source.

Some of the best article ideas are combinations of idea book entries. Let's look at the second entry in Figure 4. The focus of this idea differs little from our previous example except for the means of travel. Either one could be put through a feasibility study (see Chapter 4) and, if the idea has validity and the markets exist, become the topic of selling articles.

If you have two ideas each strong enough to warrant publication, sometimes they can be merged or aligned to create an even stronger idea. For example, why not combine backpacking, cycling, and flying? Then, depending on the markets where it is sold, you could adjust the title accordingly. For example, to a travel market where the ways of traveling are more important than the actual backpacking, you might call it "jet-biking" and focus on how one could pack a ten-speed, leave from the local airport, fly to, say, Calgary, deplane, reassemble the unpacked cycle, and pedal to Banff-Jasper, to ride in as far as possible or desired, secure the cycle, and backpack at will. Reverse the process on the return, find two or three more sites to describe in a similar fashion, and you have a story salable nationwide to travel sections of magazines and newspapers.

We have simply taken two dormant ideas from our collection, each with sale potential of its own, and combined them into a different and highly salable winner. Or three distinct sales on two ideas. A repository for capturing ideas makes such a felicitous combination far more probable.

Two final reasons an idea book makes sense, particularly for beginners: One, it forces you to do something every day to remind you that you're a writer— and may not be writing! In a way it's like forcing yourself to put on running attire every morning because you call yourself a runner. Then, as long as you're dressed . . .

And having to find three ideas a day will train you to see ideas. Which is absurd after you've been writing for a while. By then you realize that if ideas were leaves, you'd be forever buried eye deep. Professionals can think up enough ideas in an hour to last them a lifetime. But beginners don't see them that clearly. To some, if an idea were a leaf, life would be like Siberia in the winter. The idea book is the most practical way I know to improve one's vision while creating a workbook of wealth.

Make the idea book the first of seven operational steps:

1. Write your ideas in the idea book, one per page, including information you know or would like to know, slants the article might take, and possible markets.

2. As additional information becomes available, add to the idea page. This includes new sources, other potential markets, and clippings.

3. If you decide to write about the idea, conduct a

feasibility study, noting on the page the sources used (or to be used). If, during the feasibility study, you find new ideas for other articles, note them on the same page, if they are new slants to the same topic, or on a new page, if they aren't closely linked.

4. Preparing a market list will be part of the feasibility study. If the list is short, write it on your idea page. If it's long, add a second and additional pages behind your original page in the idea book and record it, to keep the information close together.

5. When you query or submit a manuscript about the idea, note it both on the idea page and your mailing record.

6. When you start gathering loose information about the idea, remove the page(s) from the idea book and transfer them to a subject folder. That usually takes place during the feasibility study or when you begin querying. Keep all correspondence and research material in that folder with your original idea page(s).

7. Keep your basic idea and research material filed by subject. When you receive a go-ahead to a query, or sell a simultaneous submission, open a different file under that publication's name. In that file keep the specific correspondence and copies of the actual manuscript, tear sheets, and other material directly related to the sale.

Is an idea book mandatory for success? Nope. Will it make you rich and famous? Hardly. Is it worth the time and hassle? You bet. Unless, of course, you're over your eyes in ideas and fully involved in bringing them to print. Everybody else: Today is the day to buy that three-ring holder and lots and lots of paper!

QUESTIONS, ANSWERS, AND ADDITIONAL THOUGHTS

Q: A single-topic idea book?

A: Why not? The idea book is to expand idea-finding skills and horizons plus strengthen discipline. But if you already know that what you want to write about—only and forever—is, say, baseball, then why not zero in from the outset? Or if you're eager to topic-spoke now, and learn the rest by the doing, why not focus your ideas from the beginning?

One way might be to break your topic into subtopics, then ask the questions that naturally flow from each. Another way would be to simply let the ideas flow, to later separate them into spokes or subtopics. Using baseball as the theme, let's see examples of both approaches:

Pitchers:

Who was the fastest pitcher of all time? Today? How do you know? Compare "junk ball" hurlers: the best knuckleball, screwball, palm ball, fork ball, etc.

Biggest screwballs on the mound—then and now.

The famous submarine and sidearm throwers in the majors: how the style affects their control, speed, length of pitching time.

Ask managers: To what degree is pitching the key to victory? Stats to prove it? Pennant winners with high team ERAs?

Umpires:

Oddities, anecdotes, tragedies, joys of major league
    umping.

Average day in life of major league umpire.

How can a person get trained if he/she wants to
    ump in the majors? Schools? Exams? Contacts
    for jobs? How fast does one rise? What are the
    top rewards?

Best and worst umps in majors, now and all-time.
    Why? Says who?

General topics:

"House characters" at the various parks: chickens,
    clowns, balls with arms and legs. Who are they
    and why are they there?

Do the teams control the diets of preseason training
    programs of their players? Curfew enforced?

Explain the detoxification program for players
    today who become drug-dependent.

Who were/are the best sign stealers? How do they
    do it? If the fans want to try, what should they
    know?

Equipment snafus: What have the teams done
    when their uniforms or players didn't make it for
    the games?

At what age can a youngster safely throw a curve or
    arm-straining pitch? Why?

Explain the difficulties baseball suffered during
    WW II. Humorous results, sad stories.

For kids thinking of a major league career, in what
    positions do they have the best chance? The
    worst?

Women in professional baseball: umps, managers, coaches, business positions? First players: when, where?

Q: 750 ideas a year?

A: Figure 52 weeks, subtract 2 of those for idle time, multiply the remaining 50 by five days per week times three ideas per day. Does it pay? Depends on what you do with the ideas. Say it takes 10 minutes each to write them in the book. (Thinking them up you do on your own time!) That's 30 minutes a day times 250 days, or 125 hours. If $5 an hour to write down ideas is a fair return, you'd have to earn back $625—make it $650 to pay for the paper and holder. About what two medium-range magazine articles pay, at $325 each. If you sell 25 articles from those ideas, it's the bargain of the year. If you never get around to using them, well, you must decide.

Q: Idea book index?

A: If you have the time and the need. In fact, for most it would illogically divert time and attention to what should be, at most, a secondary helping tool. Yet if you are an inveterate clipper and will be keeping idea books for years, this could be a godsend to help find old entries in the bulging repositories. Start it early and limit it to the title or key word(s) of the topic. If you keep it daily and you number each page successively in your books, all you need is the year, page number, and classification divided by the letters of the alphabet:

	Page	Title/Topic
	11	geraniums
	14	gunships 1812, Lake Erie
G/1983	15	Goleta/WW II attack

29   gorilla, sense of direction
33   golf tours to S.A.?
49   gill nets, sharks

Q: Where do you find the market categories?

A: The best source may be the table of contents of *Writer's Market*, since it lists by categories and it would likely be your next step anyway should you pursue the idea into print. But don't be bound by it. You can write down the kinds of people who would enjoy reading about the idea, then match them later to the kind of magazines they read.

BIBLIOGRAPHY

Burgett, Gordon. "Finding Ideas for Articles That Sell." Report, Communication Unlimited, 1987.
Burgett, Gordon. "300 Ideas for Travel Articles." Report, Communication Unlimited, 1988.

——————■——————

I think you must remember that a writer is a simple-minded person to begin with and go on that basis. He's not a great mind, he's not a great thinker, he's not a great philosopher, he's a story-teller.

Erskine Caldwell, 1958

CHAPTER 4

The Feasibility Study

A feasibility study for queried articles is the result of successfully completing numbers (2) through (10) of "How to Prepare and Market Articles That Sell," Figure 3, and follows choosing an appropriate idea or topic to write about.

The questions the study attempts to answer are plain enough: "Is it feasible to sell an article about this topic for a sufficient price?" and "Is it feasible to write the article that you promise in the query?" You never completely know the answers, though, and that's where guesswork, or a hunch, or risk, enters in.

Why do you need a feasibility study? To reduce potential time spent and to increase your selling (hence profit) ratio.

On the marketing side, the feasibility study consists of determining who would want to read about your topic, what publications they read, when and how much those publications pay, which have used the same or a similar topic recently, what other publications have also dealt with the same or a related topic, and—based on that information—which publications you should query in what order. The last is called the market list.

On the writing side, you'll want to know more about the articles in print about your topic: the facts, quotes, and anecdotes used as well as the sources for each. You'll want to know what other material is available from media and from human resources. And you'll want to know the preferred format and the target readership of the top publications on your market list.

A hard look at the market list will tell you whether the topic is worth investing the time to produce the copy. A close analysis of the research results will tell you what to promise in the query so you know what you can deliver if you receive a go-ahead from the editor.

The trick is to spend the least amount of time at the feasibility stage to extract the greatest amount of applicable material. The goal is to write a selling query letter that rings with wisdom and competence.

In the beginning, though, feasibility studies take a lot of time, because the novice is learning to use research tools and words. The time required shrinks quickly as the process becomes familiar.

What makes feasibility studies appear financially unproductive is that they are done before the writer knows whether the topic will result in a sale. Since they precede the query letter and they carry no guarantee of eventual compensation, they are a financial risk.

You may spend an hour, or eight, investigating an exciting idea only to discover that (1) no editor is interested, or (2) a hundred editors would pay a packet of Krugerrands if you could prove what you contend—but it is, alas, unprovable! Yet in time saved overall it is worth the hours gambled to make that discovery before you query.

Thus the feasibility study is a risk, consumes time, and entails work. But in the long run it is the only prudent path to follow. Without it you may sell an occasional item or even hit a rare vein of gold. But with it you should be able to turn topic after topic, shown feasible to sell and write, into reliable, steady income for as long as you persevere. And perseverance may be the sole trait shared by all professionals in the writing world.

MARKETING FEASIBILITY

1. Finding Your Readers

Assuming that you have a topic to write about, you must next find out who would buy a magazine to read what you want to write. To guide us, let's refer to Figure 3, "How to Prepare and Market Articles That Sell":

Who would benefit from reading your article?

Who would be most interested?

What kind of readers would select your specific subject from a variety of choices?

Rank all those potential readers in order, with the ones who would derive the most benefits first.

There are two ways to compose a potential readers' list: guesswork and legwork.

Guesswork is less strenuous. Look at your topic and make a note of as many ways that you could write about it as come to mind and for which, you imagine or know, enough facts or material exist for complete articles. Then ask yourself who would benefit—get rich, beautiful, happy, more secure, etc.—from reading your article. Let your mind wander (or your feet will have to). When you have run out of obvious beneficiaries, add those who would be sufficiently interested to buy a magazine to read about the topic even though the purchase would bring no direct benefit.

Legwork takes you to the library to see where this idea has appeared before. And that takes you to (2), where you find readers by what they read.

2. Matching Those Readers to What They Read

A close check of the library resources will show you where articles about or related to your topic have been published. The readers of those publications are also the most likely readers of your article.

If you are writing about the reappearance of men's hats, for example, you could either guess which magazines might run such top-flight material or you could check to see which ones have recently published articles about the topic. The best guide for commercial magazines is the *Reader's Guide to Periodical Literature*. If the topic has academic elements to it, consult one of the similar academic references.

List every article on the topic in print for at least the past three years, plus where and when it appeared, so you can find it later, if needed.

Once you have located appropriate material in specific magazines, check the index of the current *Writer's Market* to see which subject categories the magazines are listed under. Then review the other magazines in those categories to see whether they would also be logical targets for your article.

There are many magazines not listed in either the *Reader's Guide* or *Writer's Market* that also buy from the public. You would most likely find them on the magazine racks of newsstands, supermarkets, drugstores, and some bookstores; in other periodical guides and indexes at the library; and through the good graces of the reference librarian.

Check its masthead, then write or call to ask whether the publication buys freelance submissions. If so, request that a writer's guideline sheet be sent to you. The sheets generally include the same information (or more) that appears in *Writer's Market*. You can query these unlisted publications outright, of course, and take your chances, but it makes much more sense to do so knowing their policy and needs beforehand. Remember, you are selling time. Blind queries are hardly efficient.

3. Creating a Publications List

Now that you have found the most obvious markets for your topic, and have located articles about it in others, you must dig deeper both to expand those markets and to find additional research sources. The work already done, plus the expansion and modification of this step, will result in a publications list. This, in turn, will serve as the base for a market list and a later source list.

List additional words, titles, classifications, and categories under which you might find related articles, then check the library listings to ferret out more printed material. How might your topic be written differently to appeal to readers of different ages or economic status? Can it be modified for different regional uses?

Have articles about your subject appeared in the newspapers? Check the newspaper indexes at your library for the past three years or so to see what has been published and in what section. The actual copy will serve for research later; where it appeared might suggest additional sales possibilities. (The travel, food, and the op-ed sections often buy freelance submissions, and you may wish to offer articles to magazines, queried, and to newspapers, simultaneously. Or to a syndicate serving newspapers.)

When you have finished listing the articles and publications that might be interested in your work, thus expanding your publications list as far as you can at this point, you may have to reconsider some of those already listed as selling outlets. You will want to look again at each magazine that has used material about your topic in the past three years. The reason is that many, probably most, editors won't return to the same subject too quickly unless it is at the core of their publishing purpose, like a how-to gardening article in a gardening magazine.

If an article like yours was used recently, you can either wait for a reasonable length of time to pass before querying or you can change the focus of your piece to establish an obvious distance or a clearly different slant. As mentioned, three years is a rule of thumb used by many editors as the appropriate length of time before they will return to the same topic.

4. Studying Those Publications

The purpose of all this matching of readers to reading material and searching the *Reader's Guide to Periodical Literature* and newspaper indexes is to prepare a market list. The information you have gathered will help you rank the publishers on that list from the most likely (and faster/highest paying) to the least. Those unlikely to buy your opus simply won't be listed.

You need specific information about a publication to be able to fully evaluate it. The third step of "How to Prepare and Market Articles That Sell" lists seven types of information (slightly reworded below) that will help you construct and intelligently rank your list.

All or most of that information can be found in the *Writer's Market* write-ups, in the writer's guidelines sent by unlisted publications, or by reading the publication itself. Some will be specifically stated, some you can deduce or guesstimate.

Using the seven questions that follow, find the information you need and write it down so you can use it for comparison when you actually rank the market list.

Q: Does the publication pay on acceptance or publication?

A: Payment on acceptance means that the editor pays when he OKs the manuscript. The usual procedure finds you (1) querying with an idea, (2) receiving a go-ahead from the editor, (3) completing the research and writing the piece, (4) mailing it to the same editor, and (5) receiving a letter accepting the work, with payment or notice that it will be forthcoming at the next pay schedule, within 30 days.

Therefore your article need never be printed for you to be paid. You hope that it is, of course, but the payment is for your idea and its submission in printable form.

Payment on publication means that the editor does not pay until the article has been printed in that publication. In other words, "Send it to us, let us put it on our desk with the other 120 or 400 manuscripts we already have, and if we use it we will pay you." Payment *if* your manuscript somehow stays afloat in that sea of copy, *if* the editor uses it, *if* the editor remembers to pay, and *if* the publication doesn't fold.

A lot of ifs. A shaky foundation for economic survival, much less prosperity. Your article might be held six months, twelve months, two years; all are too common. You can't send it elsewhere; you can't sell reprints or rewrites. It is frozen. So being paid on publication is for losers, the desperate, or for second rights (see Chapter 5).

Q: How much does the publication pay for articles as long as yours?

A: Since you've yet to write the article and don't know its length, this question is impossible to answer. Write down the ranges for article length and pay mentioned. For example, the entry in *Writer's Market* might recommend pieces from 800 to 1,600 words for which the magazine pays $100–$350. So make two columns—LENGTH and PAY RANGE—and list each publication in this way. Imprecise as it is, you will be able to select the high payers from those eager to keep you at the poverty level.

Q: Does the publication prefer a query or a direct submission?

A: The answer is crucial if you want to move past the 75% plateau. The only justification for sending an original piece unqueried would be the possibility of simultaneous submission or a megabucks special where the $50,000 payment is worth the gamble. The *Writer's Market* entries will tell you how the editor should be approached. Remember, you can always query a publication that prefers direct submissions, but their commitment to buy, should they give you a go-ahead, may be considerably weaker than that of those accustomed to query letters. Beware.

Q: How often does the publication come out?

A: Most magazines are monthlies, so this is seldom much of a factor in ranking markets. Still, the frequency of publication directly affects the amount of copy used. Dailies use 365 times more copy, all else equal, than annuals. Some magazines—for teachers and students, for example—aren't published during the summer, so you must approach summer topics differently.

Q: What percentage of the publication is written by freelancers?

A: There are two ways to determine this percentage, or close to it. One, it might be stated in the write-ups of the publication's needs. Or you can review the masthead, note the names, and figure out what percentage of the bylined material is written by those listed. Presume the other writers are freelancers.

That percentage is important so you can identify publications that are overwhelmingly written in-house vs. those more receptive to, and more accustomed to using, outside submissions. Clearly, a magazine can have every desirable quality—wants queries, pays handsomely on acceptance, publishes often, and uses material about the subjects you know best—but if it buys only one article a year, it's hardly your long-awaited pot of gold.

Don't totally avoid those that buy rarely from outsiders but, given a choice, go where the freelance traffic is.

Q: What manuscript length does the publication prefer?

A: It might appear that this is the least important element for market ranking. After all, if it pays enough, who cares about the length?

Not quite so. For one thing, the pay often is linked to the length. And if you are querying about an in-depth, extensive exposé, it is important to know that some publications never print articles that exceed

800 words. So if your work absolutely has to be 1,800 words to make sense, length matters.

Sometimes the word count is stipulated in the write-ups; often it is too vague, or general, to be of much assistance. So count a page of the publication and make an estimate from it, then use that knowledge to determine which publications would even consider using your article if it will be exceptionally short or long.

Q: Does the publication provide additional information that will affect its placement on your list?

A: Most of this information will concern the topic itself. If your article will be written for Serbian barbers and there exists a *Serbian Barber's Magazine*, it would certainly move to or near the top of your list. Items that will positively or negatively influence the position of a market in the ranking will come from the needs write-ups, from reading the publications themselves, from gossip and fact-swapping about "hot" publications and fitful payers, and sometimes from nowhere but your own gut sense that the publication should be placed here rather than there.

5. Preparing Your Market List

Now that you have identified the readers and what they read, then gleaned essential facts about those publications, you can use that information to devise a market list that will let you query from the best sale down.

"Best" in this case means both the most desirable monetarily and the most likely to use your copy.

What criteria do you use to determine the order of your market list? There are five. The first is *when the publication pays*, on acceptance or publication. Draw a line on a sheet of paper, then place all the publications you are considering that pay on acceptance above the line and those that pay on publication below it.

The second criterion is *money*. Rank the publications from the highest payer to the lowest. Don't make earning a good wage from writing any harder than it is. Don't do what the losers do. They say, "Well, I'm a new writer, so I'll start at the bottom and work up." Think about that. If a publication paying $100 rejects your article, do you think that one paying $1,000 is going to jump at the chance to pick up the other's rejects?

Head right for the top markets. The worst that will happen is that they will say no. In the best of times, beginners aren't going to bat much better than .333 with queries. Probably worse at first. While you grow into the suit you will learn to write excellent queries—just what you need to know. And while you are learning, one of those top markets will say yes, you'll sell the article, and you'll be hooked on the writing game forever.

The third criterion in arranging your market list is the *number of issues* the publication prints a year. The fourth, the *percentage of freelance material* the publication buys. And the last, that vague *other information* and "gut feeling" category we just discussed, which should be used with caution and rarely.

Once you have the facts and have established your market list, you then use it to determine the order in which you write and send your queries. A go-ahead will then help determine which markets you'll query about the topic from a different slant or for rewrites or which will be offered reprints. In an ideal situation, every market listed will result in a sale. In a more realistic world, the list lets you direct your idea "best first." It puts order where potshots, trepidation, chaos, and blatant ignorance usually reign for the novice. It also replaces frustration with greenbacks.

WRITING FEASIBILITY

Once you have a market list (which can always be changed as new information becomes available), you need to focus on the article itself. Specifically, you need to answer the second feasibility question, "Is it feasible to write the article that you promise in the query?"

That's easy enough if you promise very little in the query. Yet to sell the idea, the query can't be too vague. It must suggest the range of the topic and include enough information—facts, quotes, anecdotes—to pique the editor's interest. No less important, it must be 100% accurate.

None of which should stump a writer. You make a practice of being accurate and filling your pages with lively, well-honed prose. The trick is to determine what you can provide in the final manuscript and find the tidbits to make the query sell in the least amount of time.

1. Reviewing Material in Print

The first thing you must do is review the published articles that you noted while preparing the market list. You are doing this for two reasons: (1) where the items are nearly identical, to see how they were organized, what sources the writers used, and how your article will differ, and (2) to extract factual material for your own query, plus identify sources for quotations: people quoted, positions or types to quote, reference books or outlets mentioned.

You don't have to read every article on the list, just those closest to what you must know or those that you think contain information needed to write the query. You'll read the others, if necessary, later when you have received a positive reply to your query and are completing the article research. In other words, at this stage you pluck what is needed; later, if there is a later with this topic, you clean the whole goose.

There is a purpose to the plucking, as we've said. A source list is where you put the feathers.

2. Compiling a Source List

To know how much you can promise about your article in your query, you need to compile a source list, much as you did a market list a while back. To the compilation you'll do now, at the querying stage, you will continue to add material if there is a next stage (and there should be, considering how deftly you're operating).

The source list might be kept on sheets of paper or index cards. It will contain the three components of all articles—facts, quotes, and anecdotes—plus their sources, plus any other general source indicated in the articles that might yield more material. The organization is yours.

In addition, check basic source material at the library. An overview of most topics can be found in an encyclopedia. The card catalog will lead you to books on the shelves, microfilm and microfiche, and any special collections. Cross-references will enlarge your findings. A check of the catalog numbers on the shelves may reveal scores or hundreds of other books about closely related subjects. These are the first steps. The reference librarian can help you expand from this point.

The idea is not to spend hours and weeks in the library but to head directly to the sources of the needed information so you can evaluate the breadth and depth of the material available about your topic. From that you can measure what you will be able to offer in the query. Common sense tells you not to offer more than you can deliver.

Some writers abhor libraries. Don't despair. Often it's possible to write and not rely on a library at all. The core of your topic could be a large corporation, a Peace Corps site in Africa, or the words of a movie star or an astronomer. Material found in a library by some may be discovered on the phone by others.

While the emphasis so far has been on fact gathering, your attention should be directed at word gathering too. Quotes bring immediacy to many articles, provide controversy, and inject a human dimension often hard to convey any other way. Review those articles to identify every person quoted or mentioned. Note their affiliation, their position, degree, or rank, why they are cited, who would have an opinion opposed to theirs, why they should be interviewed. If you need to know about them, contact the library or the public relations department where they work.

Anecdotes are harder to find, since they are usually buried among the facts or hidden in the quotes. Well chosen, though, an anecdote, "a short, entertaining account of some happening," recast in your own words, can make the difference in selling an idea through a query in much the same way a fast, direct lead can sell an article. Guard anecdotes and quotes the way politicians hoard platitudes. Nothing fleshes out a person faster than a tale told in his own tongue.

Finally, you may pull together everything known

about a subject, plus some conjecture, and still need more for a decent query, then more yet for the article to follow. The piece may depend on an interview or the results of a study. You may have to phone or write to get the assurances that your material will exist when needed, plus some information about it before the fact.

Welcome to the world of live reporting! Just keep your costs in reasonable proportion to your potential earnings, remember that what you need first is query material (about three to five paragraphs long), and keep tally of your sources just as you would with library or article-derived information.

How much source material do you need? Enough to write an accurate query letter and to know where you are headed to complete the research once you've received a go-ahead.

3. Analyzing Your Target Publications

All that remains now, before writing the query, is to adapt the material at hand about your subject to the top publication on your market list. To know what material to use, and how, you must study that publication closely to see what it buys, then offer to produce the same in your article.

The most direct way to do this is to find the last few issues of the publication and read them from front to back. At the same time, study again the entry in Writer's Market to see how closely the items in print conform to the stated needs. If they differ, how? Is that because of special circumstances—holidays, the season, some calamity like a flood or earthquake—or does it indicate a basic change in the direction of the publication?

Ask yourself who is reading that publication. The

ads tell all. The people who buy those products read those words. If they are buying round-the-world cruises and $1,000 suitcases, they are the wrong market for a live-off-the-land survival hike. A sense of the readership plus what the publication has been printing the past few months will suggest the slant or angle your article should take.

"How to Study a Printed Magazine Article," Figure 5, will be your best guide here. The most important pre-query steps are also outlined in Figure 3, "How to Prepare and Market Articles That Sell." Select two or three articles from those last issues that are closest in theme or form to what you want to write and outline them. What question does each article answer? By what steps does it get there?

Figure 5 How to Study a Printed Magazine Article

1. Read the article closely, then ask yourself what basic or working question it answers. Write the question out. It may also answer secondary questions, so write those out too.

2. Now read the entry for that publication in *Writer's Market* for the year of (or preceding) the article's appearance. Given the working question in (1) and the indications in *Writer's Market* of what that magazine was seeking, try to put yourself in the writer's shoes. How did the writer slant the subject to appeal to the magazine's readers? Why did the editor buy it? Study its length, illustrations, position in the magazine.

3. To see how the writer carries the main theme through the article, underline each word that relates directly to that theme, then outline the entire piece. Study the writer's use of facts, quotes, and anecdotes. What is the ratio between them? How is humor used? Is it spread and balanced to the same degree throughout? Do other articles in this issue use facts, quotes, anecdotes, and

humor in roughly the same way and in the same proportion?

4. List every source used, including direct references and
   quotations. Where would the writer find the facts,
   opinions, and quotes that are not clearly identified by
   source in the article? If you are uncertain, indicate
   where you would find the material—or where you
   would go to find out.

5. Focus on the quotations. Why is each used? How does
   it carry the theme forward? Note how the source of the
   quotation is introduced, and how much the reader
   must know about the source to place the person and
   what is said in perspective.

6. Is the article written in first person (I), second (you), or
   third (he, she, or it)? How does that strengthen the article? Does the person change? Why or why not? Are
   most other articles in the same issue written in the
   same person?

7. Set the title aside and concentrate on the lead. How
   long is it, in words or sentences? How does it grab your
   interest? Does it make you want to read more? Why?
   How does it compare with other leads in that issue?

8. Most articles begin with a short lead followed by a
   longer second paragraph that ties the lead to the body
   of the article. Called the transitional paragraph, it tells
   where you are going and how you will get there. It
   bridges the attention-grabbing elements of the lead to
   the expository elements of the body by setting direction, tone, and pace. Find the transitional paragraph
   and study it. Organizationally, after the lead it is the
   most important item in the article.

9. Now underline the first sentence in each paragraph.
   They should form a chain that will pull you through
   the piece. Note how the writer draws the paragraphs together with transitional words and phrases. Circle the
   words that perform this linking function. Often the
   same words or ideas will be repeated in the last sentence of one paragraph and the first sentence of the
   next.

10. Earlier you outlined the article. Now look at the transi-

tional words and the underlined first sentences and see
how the structure ties the theme together. Is the article
structured chronologically, developmentally, by alter-
nating examples, point by point? Or if the article was
written to answer the working question you isolated in
(1), did the answers to the secondary questions stem-
ming from that working question provide the article's
organizational structure?

11. How does the article end? Does it tie back to the lead?
Does it repeat an opening phrase or idea? The conclusion should reinforce and strengthen the direction the
article has taken. Does it? How?

12. Finally, look at the title. It may have been changed or
rewritten by the editor. Nonetheless, does it correctly
describe the article that follows? Does it tease, quote,
pique one's curiosity, state facts? What technique does
it use to make the reader want to read the article?

Very important is the use of humor. If a magazine
hasn't run a drop of humor, intentional or accidental,
in the past decade, the editor isn't overly receptive to
thigh-slappers. On the other hand, if every writer
seems to have written for those pages with tongue in
cheek, spare the editor your doomsday ditties. The
point: Give the editor more of what he's been buying,
to the same degree. *Mad* magazine, mad copy; a light,
fluffy publication, light fluff; pages of obvious tem-
perance, sober prose.

Even more important, what is the ratio of fact to
quote to anecdote? That ratio is as close to a telltale
footprint consistently discernible as you will find in
journalistic style.

Two examples. Scientific journals use articles that
are full of facts and heavy with quotes but are almost
devoid of anecdotes. Gossip magazines are full of anecdotes and quotes but have few facts. Publications

are remarkably consistent when it comes to their balance of facts, quotes, and anecdotes, as well as their level of humor. Find that balance, write to it, and sell, sell, sell.

This knowledge is crucial because it will determine what you will write in your query and how. Your query letter will be a preview of your article, a display of what you will write about, the examples you will use, the purpose and means, all done in the same style you will use in the final product.

When you receive a go-ahead, you will complete all 12 steps of "How to Study a Printed Magazine Article." For now, use those that give you the sense of what will be needed later, particularly (1)–(3). Then draw from your sources and find additional material to write a query that will convince the editor that the final article, if requested, will be a super addition to his pages.

Are you ready to query? Great! First we'll talk about rights, to assuage your fear that somebody is hiding inside the mailbox eager to steal your words and make a million. Then we'll tell you how those words will make that editor drool with anticipation. (You knew that editors drooled. Now you know why!)

ADDITIONAL THOUGHTS

I never realize how ignorant I am until I have to bring an idea to life in a query. Then I rediscover that what I know about the topic is only an inch more than what the readers also learned from the same books, articles, and visual media. I repeatedly feel like a born-again ignoramus.

Still, despite the fact that my ignorance is probably all-inclusive and permanent and I will never know a gnat's worth of the knowable, I still want to write for money. Furthermore, in a life already too short I'll write only about those things that interest me. Therefore, I have to find a way both to overcome my ignorance and share my interests, profitably, with others.

My way is the feasibility study. It helps me dress up naked thoughts in respectable words.

———■———

No one who cannot limit himself has ever been able to write.

Nicolas Boileau, 1674

CHAPTER 5

Copyright and Other Rights

Other than marketing, nothing is more confusing to the new writer than the issue of rights. Actually, there is little reason for bewilderment, anxiety, or even undue concern.

Two kinds of rights are involved in freelance sales. "Copyright" is one; "all rights," "first rights," "second rights" are the other. While they sound perplexingly similar, they are distinct in purpose and means of procurement. So let's discuss each separately.

But first a disclaimer. I'm not a lawyer, and if you have specific questions about any of the rights discussed, you should seek legal counsel.

Copyright seems to be the biggest bogeyman, though it's hard to see why. Nothing could be more straightforward or easier to register. Nor is any term more often misused when applied to writing. The standard question is "Did you copyright your article, script, book?" When in fact the only question is whether you *registered* the copyright, which you rarely do for articles.

What isn't understood is that in a common-law country such as ours, the rights to the copy come with its creation. As you write an article or take notes in a class, when you "fix" a mode of expression in "copy" (in our case so it can be read), that copy is "copyrighted" as it is written. The rights are automatically yours. You are creating property just as if you were sculpting a statue or painting a canvas. The rights are yours as the property is created, without need of further legal action.

Should somebody else take that property, sell it, and cause you financial damage, you could take him to court. If you could prove that you created that item, you should win. Stripped of 100 complications that nimble minds can imagine, it's as simple as that.

But if you had registered it (sent the proper forms, fee, and copies of the item to Washington, D.C.) and placed the copyright symbol on it—details to follow—your victory would be even easier. Because in the first example *you* must prove that the object was your creation. But once it's registered and properly identified, the other person must prove that *he* created the object. That's a big difference in court.

TO REGISTER OR NOT

Then why not just register and put the symbol on everything? Because the first costs money and takes time, and the second can be counterproductive. In a business sense a copyright is worth registering only when an infringement suit might be needed to protect potential earnings. Yet such a suit is expensive. Many items would never earn enough to justify going to court. So only the potentially lucrative forms of creation usually get registered: books, scripts, music, lyrics, newsletters, software for computers, etc.

As for the symbol being counterproductive, magazine editors don't expect you to copyright articles. Some are offended by the symbol and will refuse to use the material at all. They see it as one more proof of writer's paranoia, a warning from you to ensure that the editor won't use the manuscript without paying—or, horrors, shuttle it to a crony or a cousin in some remote bailiwick to somehow reap millions from it. In fact editors would be fools to put your words in print and not pay, as they know. Nor do 99% have the slightest interest in doing so.

What is the symbol and what does it mean? For literary items, it is a © followed by the date of creation and the writer's name. The symbol tells others that according to the Copyright Act of 1976 (title 17, U.S. Code) you, as the owner of the copyright, have the exclusive right to do and authorize others to do the following:

- *to reproduce* the copyrighted work in copies
- *to prepare derivative works* based upon the copyrighted work
- *to distribute copies* of the copyrighted work to the public by sale or other transfer of ownership, or by rental, lease, or lending
- *to perform the copyrighted work publicly*
- *to display the copyrighted work publicly*

For our purposes, you can register literary works, musical works (including words), dramatic works (including music), and motion pictures and other audiovisual works. But you can't register ideas, procedures, methods, titles, names, short phrases, or slogans, to select the most appropriate items related to our topic.

You don't copyright ideas. You copyright, and register if you wish, the expression of those ideas. Although you write about pet care you cannot somehow prevent others from writing about pet care, in general or particular. You have only the right to what you say about the topic: the words as used in your means of expression. Others can write about the same topic, even in a similar fashion. But they can't do it in precisely the same way, nor can they repeat or copy your writing. That right to copy is your copyright.

How do you register the copyright? In summary, you must complete the proper form and send $10 plus the stipulated number of duplicates of the item to be registered. The symbol should be affixed to the item before it is sold or distributed publicly. Then you have up to a year to complete the registration once that item is sold or distributed. In certain cases you can also include many items of a similar nature on the same form for the same fee.

CONTRACTUAL RIGHTS

Of more immediate importance are the rights that are purchased with your manuscript. Those are contractual rights. They define how often the editor can use your copy, and are part of the three-element definition of contract: offer, consideration, and acceptance.

You want to sell your writing to an editor, yet you must know what you are selling, when, and the limits to how it can be used. Copyright provides a general legal framework for your protection. The contractual rights make that specific.

You write a query letter: "Would you be interested (in buying) an article about . . .?" Or you submit a finished manuscript. Either is an offer. Consideration refers to money. Since the pay rates of most publications are listed in the current *Writer's Market*, or that information is readily available, and it is generally understood that commercial publications pay for manuscripts used anyway, consideration is generally understood as being implied in this relationship and need not be mentioned in the correspondence or transaction. (If there was any doubt at the time I was dealing with the editor, however, I'd mention it, and if doubt still persisted, get it in writing.)

What remains is the acceptance. We will discuss the various forms of acceptance and rejection later in this book, but for our needs now the editor must at some point agree that the article will be bought. Somewhere between the offer and that acceptance you should know the rights that will be purchased.

Usually that is simple. The *Writer's Market* entry will state: "all rights bought" or "we purchase North American first serial rights" or whatever. (Serial means magazine.) If that is acceptable, no mention of rights need be made in your correspondence. As long as the edition of that guide is current and the editor doesn't alter that information, you can expect those rights to be bought. (Again, if it's unclear or you want absolute confirmation, explain this to the editor.) If nothing is stated concerning the rights bought, ask.

These rights fall into three general categories: all rights, first rights, and second rights.

Many of the highest-paying publications want all rights (yet many of those will settle for first rights). "All rights" is as comprehensive as it sounds. The publication buys all the rights to what you wrote, to use as it sees fit, in the first printing, subsequent printings, anthologies, and so on. Sounds dreadful until you realize that all the editors bought was the expression of an idea in the words as written. They can make modest editorial changes in the text, but their use is limited essentially to what you provided.

They didn't buy the idea, nor can they prevent you from using that idea elsewhere in another fashion or in other words.

So all rights is far less restrictive than it implies, and usually pays the best. Don't quibble, just rewrite for other markets. The scope of change must be significant: a new title, lead, quotes, and conclusion. A better way is to find a different slant or approach and write a different article altogether. Facts are reusable, ideas can't be embargoed, and an all-rights buy can indeed be all right!

But first rights is better, since the very same article without a word's change can be sold again and again, after it has been in print. First rights entitles the editor to use the article first, which implies that it has never been in print in that form before. So you must adhere to that understanding, and by any sense of propriety, if not logistics, not offer second rights elsewhere until the piece has been published.

What do you do if an editor buys it and doesn't use it? Can you sell that manuscript again? No, you can't. But after a reasonable period of time, which could be from several months to a year, I'd contact the editor and ask when the manuscript is going to be used or whether the publication would return the rights to you. (Keep the money, though. You sold it in good faith. Their decision not to use it was just that, their decision.)

The minute a first-rights sale hits the stands, you can sell the rights again, as second rights or reprint rights. But let's save this discussion for Chapter 10, so we can clarify all the forms of resale at one time.

Just don't worry much about rights in the beginning. Worry about writing something worth stealing, then sell it.

QUESTIONS, ANSWERS, AND ADDITIONAL THOUGHTS

About Thievery and Paranoia

I oppose both! But so do editors, and that's the point of this aside. It all starts with the nagging question: What are the chances of an editor using your copy without paying you? Or of his stealing your idea and assigning it to a friend? And what can you do about it?

It happens. Copy is used and ideas stolen, but not nearly so often as the beginner's paranoia suggests. It also happens in reverse: so-called writers plucking in toto literary gems (or even rocks) and passing them off as their own. Or they sell their own copy, used, as a first-rights article without changing a word (or only a few) from the copy they had sold years ago! It's hard to tell who's ahead, editors or writers, where petty purloining is involved.

If you find yourself the victim of lifted lines, though, you want to know how to get justice *now*—or at least payment. What follows is my system, should that occur. (If you want legal help, though, see a lawyer!)

Say you send a manuscript to an editor in response to his go-ahead, receive no response to repeated letters, and discover months or years later that it was printed, without acknowledgment or payment. (You could have sent a registered letter, when the editor repeatedly ignored your letters, withdrawing the manuscript for his use. But in our case you didn't.) You have a simple recourse: Make a copy of the printed article, your original query, and the editor's go-ahead and mail them to that editor with a thank-you note, plus a reminder that the payment has yet to be received.

That should bring you a quick check and a note of apology. But if it brings silence, find out the name of the highest authority in the publishing firm, preferably the chairman of the board, and send a copy of everything you sent to the editor with an additional note that you have *still* not received payment and hope that the recipient of this second letter will be able to resolve this obvious breach of contract.

All three elements of a contract have been satisfied, yet payment has not been received. If the letter to the top honcho brings no reply, contact the Better Business Bureau. They will send you a form to complete to which you should attach a copy of all the above items. The BBB isn't a collection agency, but it does an excellent job of mediating. It will send your complaint to the company and will lend its good offices to prod them into responding.

You can also contact the postmaster at the publication's zip code and explain the situation, asking whether the firm is still in business.

If that still doesn't work, you might write to *Writer's Digest*, the monthly counterpart to *Writer's Market*, explaining what happened. If you belong to a writing organization, do the same. Both will bring your complaint to the attention of their readership. Don't forget the consumer advocate groups or representatives with the local newspaper and radio/TV stations who, by the same kind of negative publicity, get businesses to listen.

Still nothing? Small Claims Court, where you act as your own lawyer. Finally, the full lawsuit.

How frequently will you have to resort to these techniques to wrest payment from thieves? My own experience may be atypical, but of 1,000 + items in print, I have had four renegers. That's less than one-half of 1%, which is an excellent debt ratio for any business. In two cases a nudge by the BBB got me a check pronto. The other two folded with my work in their last issues. A few letters got me 17 cents of a bankruptcy settlement on a $50 claim. The other still owes me $150, a nine-year debt I may never collect.

Idea stealing is harder to prove or prevent. The problem is the gaseous consistency of ideas themselves. They can't be boxed or fenced in or even kept intact, so they can't be defined and labeled. Ideas in themselves have no legal substance. They become property when expressed in a tangible form: an article, lyrics, musical notes, etc.

And how do you prove that the editor and you didn't have the same idea at the same time? Bell and Gray not only invented telephones, completely unknown to each other, but they patented their inventions the very same day half a country apart!

So you can't overly fret at idea heisting. Think up another idea. In a week of concentrated idea-thinking you could fill a lifetime's larder. That one idea of a hundred might be swiped from a query can be exasperating, but the only sane response is one of flash anger, resignation, and replacement—to another editor—with an even better idea.

One thing is certain: If you don't risk ideas, if you don't query or write articles or books, your writing future and income will be bleak. So take the gamble. Probably 99% will be responded to, rejected, or left for you to turn into copy. Chalk up the rest to man's perversity.

Writer's paranoia can stand in the way of sensible business practices. It's a luxury few writers can afford. Concentrate on marketing good ideas, lots of them. Follow up with manuscripts so extraordinary that any editor, however larcenous at heart, will want to pay you for more.

About the Current Copyright Law

"For works created (fixed in tangible form for the first time) after January 1, 1978, the term of (copyright) protection starts at the moment of creation and lasts for the author's life, plus an additional 50 years after the author's death." (This differs for joint or group authorship and for works made for hire.)

"Under the 1976 Act, a work of original authorship is protected by copyright from the time the work is created in a fixed form; registration with the Copyright Office is not a condition of copyright protection itself (except to preserve a copyright if a work has been published with a defective or missing copyright notice), but copyright registration is a prerequisite to an infringement suit.

"To register a claim to copyright, send (1) a properly completed application form; (2) a fee of $10 (not cash) for each application; and (3) a deposit copy or phonorecord of the work being registered. The mailing address for copyright registrations is: Register of Copyrights, Copyright Office, Library of Congress, Washington, DC 20559.

"For more information about which application form to use and deposit requirements, which vary in particular situations, write to: Information and Publications Section LM-455, Copyright Office, Library of Congress, Washington, DC 20559.

"The old law required, as a mandatory condition of copyright protection, that the published copies of a work bear a copyright notice. The new enactment calls for a notice on published works, but omission or errors will not immediately result in loss of the copyright, and can be corrected within certain time limits. Innocent infringers misled by the omission or error will be shielded from liability."

Q: **How often will the editor actually change your copy?**

A: Very rarely, unless the copy is poorly written. Newspaper travel editors seem to make the most changes, probably because of space restraints. Magazine editors make far fewer changes, and the ones they do make are to streamline the piece or trim it to fit into a size format.

BIBLIOGRAPHY

Bunnin, Brad, and Peter Beren. *The Writer's Legal Companion.* Addison-Wesley, 1988.

Copyright Office, Library of Congress, Washington, D.C. 20559.

Writer's Guide to Copyright. The Writer, 1982.

------- ∎ -------

The secret of all good writing is sound judgment.

Horace, 65-8 B.C.

CHAPTER 6

Writing the
Query Letter

The query letter is the difference between the amateur and the professional in the freelance writing world.

The biggest profits come from knowing what a query letter is, how it is written, and what it must—and must not—contain. Once you've learned that, the only thing determining your selling success is your own desire and hustle.

ARTICLES

You'll notice that after-the-query writing skill is not mentioned as crucial to that success. It is important, of course, but the timing is backward. Writing skill is what makes the query work. If you can't write well enough to compose a query letter as good as the article you are proposing, there won't be any "after the query." Positive responses and subsequent sales come from query letters that sparkle, persuade, convince, reveal, expose, provoke curiosity, ignite laughter—whatever it is that the articles are to do later.

Which is a roundabout way of saying that query letters must sell an idea and you as the person to write about it, in one page of copy that makes a promise and answers key questions, with writing so clear and appealing that any editor would feel like a fool if he didn't ask to see more.

The Editor

Let's turn the tables for a moment and put you at the editor's desk to see just how the query works.

The editor, incidentally, looks just like you, except a little older and wiser in the ways of magazine needs and his boss's wants. That's right, you're the editor, but you also have a boss: the publisher, who often has bosses too. There are also other editors or their equivalents, and your scope of activity—nonfiction articles—is directly affected by their needs. One handles finances (how much to pay per article), one directs art (will you use the freelancer's photos or buy from professional stock?), another is concerned with circulation ("we need more stories about Ohio!"), still another buys fiction (which takes up your space), another sells ads, and so on. . . .

So you don't make decisions alone. In fact, every article you buy must be arm-wrestled through a meeting of all editors, then defended until the moment the piece hits the stands. As editor you must believe in the ideas you select. You must know enough about those ideas and the writers who will prepare them to fight for both. And you need reasonable assurance (and no little faith) that the writers' final manuscripts will shine in print. Why? Because your job—promotion, retention, or dismissal—is in their hands.

Therefore as editor you need reliable, knowledge-able, professional freelancers who can present excit-ing ideas that your readers want to know more about. You need six such writers a month. So you'll give eight a positive reply to their queries, knowing that one won't follow through and another will run into photo problems or give you inferior work. To compli-cate matters, you need the material in final form three months before it is read by the public, and seven months in advance for the Christmas issue.

You're at your desk on a balmy May day thinking October, fall, leaves, football, and an empty articles calendar. How are you going to fill those forlorn pages? You hardly have time to write up petty cash slips, much less investigate and pull together articles. Your assistant is even busier doing his job and the ex-tra tasks you pass his way. That's your entire staff. So where do you get October copy?

It comes through the mail. Some of it is completely written, much of it on the fringe of literacy and clearly sent to the wrong address. Those are the di-rect-submission manuscripts, the unsoliciteds, com-posed, presumably, by novices for any publication that will buy them. Surely not for your readers and al-most as surely not related to the fall or October. So they go into a huge, already bulging box to be re-turned to the misguided hopefuls when the assistant gets time or a secretary can be borrowed.

You used to feel compassion for those souls send-ing the over-the-transom pieces, with their photos and postcards and thinly veiled pleas of desperation, but after a while you wondered why they didn't even bother to read the "query first" in *Writer's Market*. And when you became editor and saw the quality of the material you needed, the quality the beginners sent, and the time it would take to find the few gems a year that might arrive by that wrong path, you gave up and turned to the high-percentage pile sent by professionals: the query letters.

So you put the unsoliciteds in the box, dump it (again) on your assistant's desk, and start through the pile of queries. Twelve today, 300 average per month—for six article slots! Some of the writers you know, most you don't. You want to print new names each month so your pool of writers will continue to expand. You try to read with an open mind.

What are you looking for? Quick, sharp letters, preferably a page but two maximum and those well worth the extra reading, that tell you (1) what the writer wants to write about, (2) how that will be done or what the article will contain, (3) whether the piece will be straight or humorous, (4) why your readers would be interested, if it's not obvious, (5) the writer's qualifications or expertise, if necessary, (6) whether the person has been in print before and where/when, and (7) whether photos are available, if needed.

The writing in the letter will be almost as important as the content: Does it show attention to accuracy and detail, is it both interesting and to the point, can the person write to the level of your magazine? If you can't tell that from the query, you will want a copy or tear sheet of a recent article that the person has had in print, to settle your doubt.

How many provide you with enough of those elements to be able to judge their ideas and writing skill? From 300 queries, maybe 50. Add 10 more to that total from whom you've bought before and who needn't convince you anew that they can write. That gives you 60 potential articles from which you must ferret out the best 8 for positive replies. (The assistant gets to reject the other 240, though you write a personal note on some of the best, encouraging them to query again.)

By what process do you eliminate 52 potentially salable articles? The appropriateness of the idea for October. (After all, a professional should know that you program some two to four months in advance.) How recently you used that or a similar idea on your pages. (Again, easily checked.) The reliability of the letter writer to produce solid, top-quality copy. (Those who have sold to you before have the edge here; the others must be judged by the query or copies of recent items in other publications they cite or send with the letter.)

From 52 to 15. Now come the toughest decisions. Much of the selection is intuitive: you like an idea and the way it is presented. The writer has a feel for the subject and can use words. The query gives you something to work with and defend in committee. The whole thing has a professional tone to it, and although the writer isn't known to you and hasn't much of a selling record so far, you're willing to take a gamble.

Others come from veterans who gave you excellent work earlier, or from experienced writers who show a firm grasp of their topics and the ability to bring that alive on your pages. Two others, unknown to you, are on the edge of the pack, but their queries are well written and the topics could leap off the page if well handled. You phone one to ask about a point made in the letter, and to listen to how clearly the person thinks. You like the responses and add her to the go-ahead list. On committee day you add the other one too, but with deeper reservations.

And thus your sojourn as editor comes to an end. (The other editors, in a surprising show of confidence, accepted all of your article picks. The results?

Two superb pieces—including one from that last candidate about whom you had the deepest reservations—four solid articles, one sent nothing, and a veteran offered a once-over-lightly disappointment that had to be returned.)

Figure 6 A Successful Article Query

1234 Fifth St.
Santa Maria, CA 93456
(805) 555-5555
March 2, 1974

Mr. Robert H. Rufa
Managing Editor, *Travel*
Floral Park, NY 11001

Dear Mr. Rufa:

You got trouble, friend,
Right here, I say,
Trouble right here in River City!

River City exists! It's hiding in north-cental Iowa much as Harold Hill described it in Meredith Willson's smash hit *The Music Man.*

The trouble, you recall, was the billiards hall, the Pleazol, and the path to salvation was a marching band, instruments bought sight unseen from the same Harold Hill.

If you go to Mason City today, walk north on Federal Avenue from Central Park, and look down you will see, in marble for all time: PLEAZOL! Alas, times change. The pool hall has moved four doors away. There's *still* trouble in River City!

I'd like to take *Travel* readers back to "River City" to see the source of so much fun. Seventy-six trombones still play to tapping feet somewhere in the world every night, 25 years after the musical made its debut!

We'll visit Meredith Willson's home town, walk the streets and talk with "plain men, modest men," then cross the bridge to see Marion the Librarian's old haunt (now housing

Iowa Kempfer Mutual Insurance) or where Marion (Meredith's mother) lived, close to Willow Creek, the "river" of River City.

What's more, since *Travel* pieces include the surrounding area, we'll visit the Hobo Center of America, the "Little Brown Church in the Vale," the site where the 4H emblem originated, fossil beds throughout the region, a buffalo preserve, the only known habitat of a rare relict mouse, Hamlin Garland's home—the kinds of places one finds in the country Midwest.

I've been in print 350 times, in travel, humor, and general interest. I'm not tooting my own horn, just Willson's flute as he did at the Cerro Gordo Hotel for the Kiwanis Club on a Wednesday afternoon in 1912. That's how it all began for him in Mason City.

Interested? I can also provide "24 made-to-order 35 mm slides as pretty as the American flag on the Fourth of July," as Harold Hill would say. A bit corny, but that's Iowa.

Gordon L. Burgett

The Query That Gets You Chosen

Writing the query letter that gets you the go-ahead takes hard work, editing and reediting, plucking and adding, until you have touched every needed point and have shown that you can write clearly and well. No magic. Nothing the average literate person with a good idea can't do. Even luck isn't much of a factor. Having a good idea and presenting it thoroughly are.

The query is written in business letter form: no indentations to start the paragraphs, single-spaced except between paragraphs, and a colon after the salutation. It is a business letter. A sales letter. You are selling your services to prepare an article about an idea you think the recipient editor's readers will buy. So the letter is businesslike in both form and tone.

That doesn't mean stiff and humorless. It means that the letter is written for a purpose, to sell an idea and you as the person to write about it. So the tone of the letter must be chosen to best help you realize your purpose. If the article is to discuss training techniques for guard geese and it is to be humorous, a humorous letter will best show the editor that you can write what you propose. Yet it must also meet all the other criteria that are necessary to receive a positive reply to your query.

What are those other criteria? We mentioned them earlier, but let's elaborate more fully now.

1. What do you want to write about? What is the purpose of the article? What is the topic? What working question does it answer? Nothing is more important than a tight, clear focus. The lack of focus, in perception or explanation, may account for more query rejections than all the other criteria combined.

Put in other terms, after reading your query and giving you a go-ahead, does the editor know precisely what you will prepare and submit? If not, no editor who wants to remain one will give a positive reply. At best the editor will ask for a clarification. Almost all will reject. So zero in, "an article about . . .," with details and slant and clarity. Don't offer an editor five choices; pick the best idea, develop it, and query. Don't offer generalities, expecting the editor to find the particulars. Focus, finish the feasibility study, and sell.

2. What will the article contain? How will you develop your idea? How will you expand the focus?

Will the core of the piece be an in-depth interview, or perhaps a series of short interviews, each approaching the theme from a different angle? Will it be an exposition of all known facts? Or an exposé of other facts too little known? Will the piece move from the general to the specific? The reverse?

To be sold, editors must know more than the mere topic. By knowing how a subject will be presented, the editor can judge the depth of preparation required, the worth of the work, and whether you have the skill and background to deliver the goods.

3. Will the article be straight or humorous? Light or tongue-in-cheek? This will depend on the topic and the publication. Some topics aren't essentially humorous: death, loneliness, starvation. Others defy serious treatment. But the most important determinant will be the ratio and degree of humor used by the publication itself, which you can check during the feasibility study.

If the treatment will be straight, then write your query letter in that manner. If humorous, write the query with the same degree of humor you would use in the final article. Also mention that the piece will be written humorously so the editor will realize that the humor was intentional, not simply the product of a good mood or favorable moon.

4. Why would the readers be interested in your article? The answer is often obvious and needs no elaboration in the query. If you are telling how to irrigate rutabaga and the magazine is for gardeners (with strange taste), the subject sells itself.

Yet there are times when you are more familiar than the editor with the tie-in. Without a short explanation or bridge between your idea and the editor's readers, your query would automatically be put in the reject pile. You may have inside information or know of new uses or demands for products, or be aware of a coming trend. If there's a chance the editor may not know, a sentence or two can create sales where rejections are otherwise certain. Rutabaga irrigation won't sell to health magazines, but if you stressed (if it were true) that rutabagas are a cure for rheumatism, with a reslanting they may indeed want this piece.

5. What are your qualifications for writing this article? That you are bright, literate, eager to gather information and able to impart it with vigor and accuracy is plenty for most pieces not requiring special skills or training. In those cases you needn't dwell on your qualifications, just show your research and writing abilities in the query.

But if the article would have better acceptance by the editor and readers if it carried the authority of having special skills or knowledge, you must either have and display them or be able to borrow them. If you're writing an article about brain surgery, for example, and you are in fact a brain surgeon, mention it in the query. But if you are a tree surgeon, mum's the word. Rather, indicate that the article will be based on an interview with a brain surgeon or two or five, enough to infuse the piece with the facts and insight gained from their learning and experience.

There are very few articles you can't write for print by borrowing others' knowledge. Just make sure the editor knows where the needed expertise in the piece is coming from.

6. Where and when have you been in print before? The stopper. If you haven't published before, who will give you your first chance? The Catch-22, the insurmountable hurdle of needing experience to gain experience, a circle without a starter's toehold.

In fact, it's far less dire than all that. You can either

gather experience and inch upward or you can write a query letter so well researched at the feasibility stage and so well composed that the editor, seeing your ability to use the skills vital to writing salable articles, gives you an opportunity.

If you opt to gather experience before querying, start with simultaneous submissions. They generate many sales quickly and fill your sails with confidence in the shortest amount of time. Then branch off from the same topics, find angles of particular interest to specific magazines, and learn the querying process. At the same time write letters to the editor, articles for the local weekly or nearby college newspaper— anything to get in print with good copy.

Alas, none of this lower-level preparation will be mentioned in your query unless it is impressive. So why do it? To give you the courage to query the top publications, and the self-assurance that, if given a go-ahead by a top payer, you can provide what you promise. The danger of working up is that it can take forever, if you let it, and that your courage will develop far more slowly than your competence.

What do you mention in the query about previous publication? Enough to impress, nothing more. If it was in the *Church Bazaar Gazette* and you are querying *Esquire*, you'd best leave it out. But if you are querying *Travel and Leisure* and you have had travel pieces in four large-city newspaper travel sections, mention it.

Another way is to use numbers: "I've been in print 200 times, including x, y, and z." That is particularly effective when your earliest experience has been at the newspaper level, where every item you wrote counts, no matter how short. Also, if you sell simultaneous submissions, are syndicated, or have an extensive reprint tally, numbers add up quickly. The stipulated publications, then, would be either the best known or most prestigious in the particular field you are querying.

A final suggestion might be to put the spotlight on the last item you wrote for publication. "My most recent article is in the current issue of _____." If it's well done (and why would you mention it if it wasn't?), include a copy of the printed piece with your query. This is particularly effective if your credits aren't overwhelming. You are saying "This is what I'm producing now. I want you to read it to see that I can write for your pages." Let the article do the selling.

7. Do you have photographs to help sell the article? If so, mention them. Don't include them with the query letter. Force the editor to ask to see them. Why? Because you are querying to sell an idea and your follow-up writing. If the photos you send with the query aren't acceptable, the editor may assume that your writing will be of the same caliber. Sell your best product—writing. If you can provide photos later, more gravy.

The more the magazine pays, the less likely it is to buy your photos or to expect you to be equally adept at both skills. The category most apt to want to see what you have is travel, where available prints or slides of little-known or remote sites may be hard to obtain.

Check the publication's photo credits to see whether the author or some other person or agency provided them, and draft your query accordingly. If you don't have photos or ready access to some of professional quality, say nothing at all.

Once written, does your query pass these four tests?

1. Is it the kind of letter a professional would write?
The key word is *professional*. Or did you dash it off
during commercials? Does it explain your idea so the
editor knows precisely what you will deliver? Is it interesting? Do you sound knowledgeable and enthusi-
astic about the topic? Does it need more editing?

2. Is it brief, complete, clear, and positive? *Brief*:
usually no longer than a page to sell an article, two
pages (with attachments) to sell a nonfiction book.
The exceptions had better be just that.

Complete: a full page, not a sentence or a paragraph. Too short and the editor will surely suspect
that (1) you can't write and are showing just the minimum to hide the fact, or (2) you don't know much
about the topic and are sending around some 10-
minute, low-risk feelers. The query letter is your
chance to parade a page of top-flight thinking and
writing; it's your setup session before the big-bucks
sale. Why would you skimp on copy when it's hard
enough to succeed using all the space at your dis-
posal?

Clear: If "clear" isn't, our problems are too large for
this tome!

Positive: You're selling an idea and yourself. Inject
negatives and you increase the slope and height of the
mountain. The writing world is already tough enough
climbing. Why make it harder?

3. Does it show attention to accuracy and detail?
Editors love both. Accuracy is the root word of continued sales. And detail, well ordered, is the difference between an empty hall and a lovely room. Both
should show in a query. Accuracy extends to spelling
and grammar. If you're too lazy to consult a diction-

ary or read your letter with a sharp eye, what will the final manuscript be like?

4. Is it convincing that the article should be written?
It is a sales letter—soft sell, of course, but sell nonetheless. The editor must want to know more from the same good source. You must be convinced that the article is worth doing, and that conviction must show in the query.

NONFICTION BOOKS

Query letters for nonfiction books differ from queries for articles, though more in scope and depth than in structure or intent.

In both kinds of query you have an idea you wish to sell to an editor, and the letter is sent to explain that idea and to propose yourself as the person to write the copy. Yet with a book there is more at stake—the publisher's money and much more of your time—so the query has a bigger sales job to do. To do it, the letter will be twice as long, with important attachments.

Whereas an article query should be limited to a page (or at most two), book queries should be held to two. The seven questions the article query must answer are even more important here.

Some inclusions, though, such as your previous items in print, may call for a complete list, which in turn might become an attachment if it runs longer than a paragraph or two. Your qualifications may have to be explained in greater depth too, and might also be best presented as a résumé.

Figure 7 Sample Book Query

1234 Fifth St.
Santa Maria, CA 93456
(805) 555-5555
Oct. 10, 1983

Mr. Robert Litsinger
Editor, Adult Books, Trade Division
Justin Winchell Press, Inc.
312 Madison Avenue
New York, NY 10017

Dear Mr. Litsinger:

I'm 45 and one of my earliest memories was seeing a trico-
lored collie bound across a school yard into the out-
stretched arms of Roddy McDowall in *Lassie Come Home.*

Millions of kids later saw *The Incredible Journey,* and who
hasn't seen, read, or heard accounts of dogs and cats finding
their way home over incredibly long distances without as
much as a push in the right direction, much less a map or
compass?

In the cases cited it was easy. Their authors wrote them
home without a whit of concern about the "how."

Yet how do you account for Bobbie, a large tawny and white
collie/English sheep dog that traveled a well-documented
3,000 miles from Indiana to Oregon in the dead of winter?
Or the several dozen other true accounts that make Lassie
look like a neighborhood stroller?

Even more puzzling are those critters who follow their mas-
ters into areas they have never seen before, covering hundreds and even thousands of miles to bark or meow on the
doorstep of the master who moved and left them behind.
They are called psi-trailing cases, and 15 of the best proven
would be woven into the text, as reported by the "father of
parapsychology," Dr. J.B. Rhine, with his daughter, Sara
Feather.

How the question the book poses would be answered is
shown in both the outline and reference/resource sheet accompanying this letter.

An example of my writing is, likewise, enclosed. Called
"Lassie," the article appeared in *The National Weekly* on
Dec. 17, 1982. Reprints or rewrites of this piece have also

appeared in *The Animal Parade, Lights Out!*, and *Fun with Animals.*

The widespread interest in the subject is shown by the number of editors eager to print this and related articles. The book proposed would build on that interest, and would explore the subject to a greater depth than is possible in one or a series of articles.

I have written two books: *The Query Book* (1980) and *Ten Sales from One Article Idea: The Process and Correspondence* (1981). In addition, I have edited six more and had 900 articles in print, in both magazines and newspapers, primarily in general interest, humor, travel, and running. A copy of either book as well as a publications list will gladly be sent, with copies of the tear sheets of the listed items that you subsequently request.

If I had in mind the definitive scientific study of animal orientation I would be the wrong writer. You'd need a "name" in zoology or animal behavior. I propose a more general book, one that looks with layman's eyes at an issue of immense curiosity, then attempts to answer all the questions the everyday reader would ask the scientists or parapsychologists. That's the point where my four college degrees and background in historical and linguistic research become useful, to ferret out the answers and translate them into clear, fluid prose.

What I hope to do with this query is ascertain your interest in the topic and me as its author, and offer to send three chapters—IA, IIA, and IIIB1—to stimulate contract talks.

Lassie had it easy. A thousand miles, some Scottish moors, a few lochs, Rollie and Tinker, and it was home, to Roddy, print, radio, TV, and "America's best loved pet."

I'll be happy if Uncle Sam will just get this letter across the U.S.! Alas, do miracles happen twice? Could it wend its way 3,000 miles, over mountain, plain, and Ohio, to the loving hands of a far-sighted, pet-loving publisher eager to give its contents a happy home? The SASE will tell all!

Regards,

Gordon Burgett

cc: outline
    reference/resource sheet
    article, "Lassie"
    SASE

But most of the letter will focus on the subject, why it should be written in book form, the angle or approach you will use, how that would differ from those of other books or articles currently in print, and why you believe readers would care enough about the volume to buy it. Your ability to write book-level prose will be judged, first and most importantly, by your writing in the query.

Attachments to the Book Query

What kind of attachments should you append to the book query? Perhaps a *synopsis* but surely a *table of contents* and a *reference/resource* page, and others as needed: a credit list of your publications, a résumé focusing on your qualifications to prepare the book, even a list of available photos (your own or where others' might be obtained). Each time you add an attachment you should refer to it in the query letter by number and title.

A synopsis of the book's contents is often the core of the query letter itself, but if the general summary is incomplete or too fragmented, an appended synopsis no longer than a page, single-spaced, is a valuable selling tool.

A table of contents shows the framework of the book. It outlines the order you will impose on the subject's development. Will the material be presented chronologically? Or will you start with one fact, add another, bring in a third, and so on? Is it to be a series of examples tied together at the beginning and end? Whatever the format, a table of contents shows that rather than a fleeting thought quickly rushed to pa-

Figure 8 Sample Book Outline

WORKING OUTLINE: *THE LASSIE PHENOMENON*

 I. The Lassie Phenomenon: How do pets find their homes/masters over long distances?
   A. Fiction: *Lassie, The Incredible Journey*
   B. Fact: historical examples and proof
   C. Fact: psi-trailing examples and proof

 II. Why do they do it?
   A. Homing: pets
   B. Survival/reproduction: wild animals

 III. How do they do it?
   A. Dogs/cats
      1. survive in the wild?
      2. five senses
      3. psi
   B. Possible explanations in other animals
      1. echolocation (see below)
      2. electricity: fish, eels
      3. avian grid: bees, pigeons, birds
      4. magnetic field: pigeons, robins, termites
      5. bacterial compass: pigeons and bees

 IV. Conclusion
   A. Summary of what is known, studies under way
   B. A sixth sense—or more?
   C. One explanation or many?

per, you have a reasoned, developed idea, like the frame of an exciting new house. All that delays its completion and sale is a publisher to underwrite its financing.

Figure 9 Sample Book Query Reference/Resource Sheet

Resources/References: THE LASSIE PHENOMENON

Resources

Animal orientation is an active field of research. Many of the scientists who have made the key discoveries related to our subject are still living. Interviews with them, and others whose names will emerge from those interviews and further research, constitute the prime resources for *The Lassie Phenomenon:*

Konrad Lorenz: pioneer in modern ethology whose concept that an animal's behavior is a product of adaptive evolution won him the Nobel Prize. His book *Man Meets Dog* explains homing. M.D., Ph.D. from the University of Vienna; currently at Max Planck Institut, Germany.

J.B. Rhine: the "father of parapsychology" and director of the Institute for Parapsychology at Duke University. His article (written with his daughter) "The Study of Cases of 'Psi-Trailing' in Animals" is the core of our book's theme. Author of *Extrasensory Perception* and *Parapsychology, Frontier Science of the Mind.*

Donald Griffin: explained the riddle of echolocation and bats in *Listening in the Dark* and *Echoes of Bats and Men.* Professor of animal behavior and comparative physiology at Rockefeller University, Griffin's specialties are the sensory basis of animal orientation, acoustic orientation, and bird navigation.

Michael Fox: a veterinarian with doctorates in science and medicine. His books *Understanding Your Dog* and *Behavior of Wolves, Dogs and Related Canines* and position as director of the Institute to Study Animal Problems, for the U.S. Humane Society, are central to this book's interests.

William Keeton: author of *Biological Science* and pro-

---

fessor at Cornell University. Keeton's specialties
are homing behavior (mainly of pigeons) and evolu-
tionary biology, with particular emphasis on the
roles of geographic and behavioral isolation in process speciation of animals.

Maurice Burton: top advocate of a "sixth sense or
more" in animal navigation, the British zoologist
wrote the recent, extensively researched The Sixth
Sense of Animals.

Ronald Lockley: English naturalist and author of
Animal Navigation. Lockley also wrote Ocean
Wanderers; The Migratory Sea Birds of the World;
and Whales, Dolphins, Porpoises.

References

The key reference books below exclude those mentioned above or other books by the same authors,
which would naturally be included where the material pertains to our topic:

Burnford, Sheila. The Incredible Journey.
Buytendijk, Frederik. The Mind of the Dog.
Carthy, J.D. Animal Navigation.
Knight, Eric. Lassie Come Home.
Matthews, G.V.T. "The Sensory Nature of Bird Navi-
gation."
Milne, Lorus and Margery. The Senses of Animals
and Man.
Pratt, J.G. "Testing for an ESP Factor in Pigeon Hom-
ing."
Slaughter and Walton. About Bats.
Topsell, Edward. The Historie of Foure-Footed
Beasts.

A reference/resource sheet helps convince the editor, representing the publisher, that your book will
have substance, that it will grow from solid research
roots.

Rarely is a book unrelated to an existing body of knowledge and experience. The editor wants to know where the facts, quotes, and anecdotes on your pages will come from. Thus a list of the "dead" (reference) and "living" (resource) fonts will be valuable to get you a go-ahead. The list will show your familiarity with the general academic texts, papers, and authorities in the field and how they relate to what you will prepare.

The reference section of your reference/resource sheet should include the key books and articles in print that you will use in a substantial way in preparing your book. Cast this section in annotated bibliography form, with the annotation showing how you will use the published material in your book. The resource section should include the names of the people you will interview or who will somehow play a direct role in your book's contents, identified by their current position or affiliation, the source of their expertise, why they are being consulted, etc.

Finding Markets and Sending Chapters

Specific information about nonfiction book publishers is contained in the "Book Publishers" section in the current *Writer's Market*. The question is which of the publishing houses listed is the best market for you. The answer comes from a feasibility study, which you must do here too, though with obvious modifications.

Write down all the ways your book might be listed in the card catalog at the library, then visit both a major university library and a town counterpart to find the full complement of academic and popular books in that field. Check the catalog at each to find books similar to your own, keeping a tally of the number of books printed by each publisher.

That list should be your marketing guide. If you are writing about ear infections, for example, your best bet will be the publishers already selling to the medical field. They have the sales contact already established. If that seems obvious, beginners by the drove avoid the obvious because they don't want to compete with, in this case, the veteran medical writers already printed by those firms. So they try publishers turning profits with books about earwigs, earrings, or ears of corn.

Check your list of the top-selling publishers in your field against their *Writer's Market* write-ups, and rearrange it in the order that best serves your needs, as discussed in Chapter 4. Then query one editor at a time, sending your letter, the attachments, and an SASE.

When you receive a go-ahead, usually you submit some representative chapters. A contract usually follows approval of those sample chapters. Payment is generally made upon chapter approval, again upon delivery of the final draft, and finally when the book is printed, or some variation of that format. That payment is an advance, say $5,000, against the royalties which are a percentage of the book's list or net price. Cloth royalties are often 10%–15%; paperback, 5%–8%.

Only when the book is very short, usually for new readers or lower primary school use and less than 50 pages long, are you asked to submit the full book for evaluation. You must decide whether the greater time involved is worth the risk.

Done as just described, nonfiction book writing is relatively no riskier than articles. Though books take more time, the payoff is bigger.

QUESTIONS, ANSWERS AND ADDITIONAL THOUGHTS

Q: Isn't it easier just to self-publish?

A: Publishing your own book can be far more time-consuming and riskier financially than having an established firm do it. Yet it can be many times more profitable, too, if you have a salable idea and market it well.

A book I just self-published tells where doing it yourself does make the most sense. Called *Self-Publishing to Tightly-Targeted Markets*, it advises you to write to a specific audience about a need they want met now.

An excellent how-to book describing the process, particularly the technical steps of putting the book together, is Dan Poynter's *The Self-Publishing Manual*, self-published, of course, by Para Publications, P.O. Box 4232, Santa Barbara, CA 93013.

Instead of the standard 10%–15% royalties, you make 100%—after costs, time, and risk. The most lucrative areas are nonfiction how-to books. The least profitable are fiction, poetry, and mass-market panaceas. Success usually comes from finding a need in a tightly identifiable market, meeting that need in print, and selling specifically to that market, plus libraries.

Most failures come from poor marketing, invisible distribution, underfinancing, insufficient profit margin in the book cost, overprinting the first edition, and amateurish packaging. Alas, rare are those who are able to write well enough to publish and market well enough to profit. So publishers do the latter, fitfully in many cases, while writers attempt the former.

Self-publishing, then, should be looked at with a hard eye before you invest your money. If none of the established publishers is willing to invest in your idea and prose, where they gain the lion's share of the profits when the product sells, there may be a reason for you to likewise be cautious before investing. Still, some do hit gold digging in what seem to others to be barren hills.

I would stay away from vanity press publishing, however, where a firm will publish your work as long as you make a major investment in its production.

Q: Should a résumé accompany your query?

A: Everything you send with that query either enhances or diminishes the idea's salability. Generally a résumé is a distraction, because it covers your entire past. If you want to send a résumé, isolate those elements that particularly qualify you to write the article. Why not include those in the query? Then if the editor wants to read a résumé, believe me, he will ask. Or you can offer to send one, if the editor is interested. Keep the focus on the query itself.

Q: What is an SASE?

A: SASE means a self-addressed, stamped envelope. You should enclose an SASE with any correspondence or submission, like queries or manuscripts, that you want back or to which you want a reply. Send an SASE until the editor tells you it's no longer necessary—a comment, in most cases, you will never receive. Be sure the envelope is large enough to hold the manuscript in the manner you want it returned (single-folded, unfolded, etc.). U.S. stamps are ill received by foreign postal exchanges, so when you are sending material beyond our national borders, send a self-addressed envelope without a stamp, hoping the recipient will attach one, or include an international reply coupon, which you can buy at your post office.

Improving Your Querying Odds

Having your material tied up for three months is the fast road to bone banquets. The way to avoid this predicament is to have many queries in circulation at the same time, all of course proposing different articles. If you have a minimum of 10 query letters out at any one time, which is both possible and advisable, 1 out of 10 floating in manuscript limbo isn't as devastating.

New Writers and Assignments

Newcomers to the writing world almost never get assignments, nor should they expect them. Yet you will hear others say that you should never write without an assignment. That's the fastest way to guarantee that you'll never write. Forget about them in the beginning. Send super queries, provide copy that is good or better than what's promised, and you'll have no problems.

———■———

What is written without effort is in general read without pleasure.

Samuel Johnson, 1709-84

CHAPTER 7

Writing the Simultaneous Submission Cover Letter

A simultaneous submission cover letter plays a less crucial role in selling your writing than the query letter. That's because it accompanies the actual manuscript, which is what the editor will use as the basis of a buying decision.

The function of the cover letter is to introduce the copy, display a sample of its contents and flavor, discuss available illustrations, perhaps talk about the rights offered, suggest other elements you could write to enhance the article, and tell whether you want the manuscript back.

Simultaneous submission cover letters are sent in six selling situations, and derivations of them: with multiple submissions sent to editors of newspaper travel sections, newspaper weekly supplements, religious magazines, regional publications, in-flight magazines, and to sell reprints.

They also come in two sizes: short and full page. Let's discuss when and why each might be sent, and what it would contain.

THE SHORT COVER LETTER

The short letter physically covers most of the top half of the front page of the manuscript, as seen in Figure 10. Its purpose is to convey the bare essentials while drawing the editor's eyes down to the text, to be enchanted by the words and images and, in one motion, send it off to be printed and the SASE to you with a hearty cheer of acceptance!

The cover note sent to Morris Rosenberg, of the *Washington Post*, has six functions, all to be done in about 5" of space. One, to tell him who I am, so I type my name at the top and sign it below, the first because of the likelihood that he can't read the second.

Two, to tell him where I live so he will send the check to that address. Three, how he can reach me by phone if there is something he wants to discuss—or photos he wants sent by express.

The fourth point is the most important: What is the copy about? He's busy. He might read a full manuscript anyway. But here I summarize the contents in the same tone in which the article is written, to save him time and to pique his curiosity. My hope is that he won't worry about points five or six now but rather will let his eyes leap to the lead and get into the text itself. If that happens, the chance of his buying is excellent. Which is precisely why I send him the shorter version of the cover letter, to let his eyes roam unimpeded. Note that the short letter obscures no text, only the title (included in the letter) and my byline.

The fifth point is also important. If you have photos or other illustrations, here is where you make their availability known, the quantity that you can provide, and how you will send them. Since my photos are seldom so extraordinary that one or several will, in

Figure 10 Sample Short Simultaneous Submission Cover Letter

1200 words

GORDON BURGETT
1234 Fifth St.
Santa Maria, CA 93456
(805) 555-5555

Dear Mr. Rosenberg:

"The Land of the Music Man" is a tree-lined Main Street in Iowa called Mason City where Meredith Willson grew up, was raised by "Marion the Librarian," played pool at the Pleazol (with its name still in marble on the sidewalk), and used a bridge immortalized by the musical/movie to go to school. The article attached tells what the Washingtonians would find today, unchanged, in the setting should they head west for a visit. . . .

I have 36 good-to-excellent b/w's available to select from, if interested—or I can send the five best.

Please don't return the ms, just your verdict in the SASE.

Thanks.

LAND OF THE MUSIC MAN
by Gordon Lee Burgett

You can almost hear and see a high-stepping, brass-buttoned, marching band triumphantly—if a bit atonally—cross that footbridge and sound those unforgettable opening notes of "Seventy Six Trombones," for River City is alive and throbbing in the heart of America's cornbelt.

It's really Mason City, a tree-lined main street of 32,000 in north-central Iowa, and it's where Meredith Willson (with two "l's," mind you) grew up, premiered musically one Wednesday afternoon before the Kiwanis Club at the still-operating Cerro Gordo Hotel, and left to play piccolo with Sousa and flute with Toscanini.

themselves, sell the story, it is enough to offer the lot to be reviewed. But if I had a super photo, here is where that would be explained, with this paragraph larger and the first, smaller. Or they would change places, giving prime attention to the photo(s) and less to the supporting copy.

Item six concerns the return of the manuscript. If I pay the postage to get it back, what will I get for my money? A folded, probably marked text that I couldn't send to another editor. So why spend the cash? I'd rather include an SASE that is too small to contain the manuscript, like a #9 envelope, with one stamp just to receive the verdict. Or a postcard with boxes to check, like

☐ Am holding for use on _____.
☐ Am holding for possible use.
☐ Sorry, can't use this article.
☐ Send your b/w's for selection.
☐ Send your best five b/w's, with negatives.
☐ Comments: _____

Can you include anything else? Sure, it's your letter. The purpose is to sell the manuscript attached, so what goes in the cover note and in what order is up to you. But what has worked for me best is displayed in Figure 10. How well has it worked? The manuscript was sent to 13 newspaper travel editors with an individual note. Nine bought it, including the *Washington Post*. And 5 bought photos.

THE FULL-PAGE COVER LETTER

If you simply can't convey the message in a short note, or you are submitting simultaneously to magazine editors (whose pace is a bit less hectic), the full-page letter probably works better.

In the first two or three paragraphs I sell the copy, and the rest looks much like the shorter note—but longer. The advantage? More space to laud the virtues of the piece or the photos. And you can use a full letterhead, if you wish.

For reprints, explained more fully in Chapter 10, the longer letter is virtually mandatory, because you have more to say. In the third paragraph I usually include the three elements necessary to selling reprints (or second rights): who bought the first rights, when the piece appeared in print, and what rights I am selling to the editor to whom I am sending the letter.

In a subsequent paragraph in the reprint cover letter I then talk about the availability of photos used in the article attached, assuming they were sold on a one-time-rights basis. I also offer the editor an opportunity to buy the photos or slides that were not purchased for the first article, and tell how I will send them.

Again, the whole idea is to sell the article that accompanies the cover letter. The size and order of contents are solely related to that function. Which prompts a final thought: The writing in the cover letter must be as sharp, enticing, and appealing as that of the article it is selling. An inferior cover letter is like a shirtless, shoeless Mercedes-Benz salesman.

———■———

*Writing comes more easily if you have
something to say.*

Sholem Asch, 1955

CHAPTER 8

Responding to the Replies

When can you expect a response from your query or direct submission? When should you get worried? How do you read the editors' replies? Does the form of response indicate whether you are close to a sale or 100 miles at bay?

DIRECT OR SIMULTANEOUS SUBMISSIONS

Let's dispose of direct or simultaneous submissions first, since there is little mystery about their exchange. *Writer's Market* or the writer's guideline sheet that the publication may have sent you (in response to your request) indicate when you can expect a reply. That reply will be yes, it's bought or being held for use; no, with or without additional comment, or maybe, with some indication of what must be done to make the piece acceptable: new lead, a rewrite, more facts, whatever.

If you haven't heard anything by the time you should have, give the editor several more weeks and send another copy of the same manuscript plus a note indicating when the piece was originally sent and saying perhaps it was lost in the mail, so you are offering another copy for the editor's consideration. Another SASE too. Usually you should wait at least two months before sending this second manuscript.

One month later and still no reply, put a black star by that publication on your list, forget it, and submit to another in that area of circulation—just as you would do if it had been rejected. That's it. Direct and simultaneous submissions are rather uncomplicated yes-no affairs worth pursuing on a volume (simultaneous) basis, for reprints, or where you have no other choice, as is the case with humor.

REPLIES TO YOUR QUERY LETTER

Query responses are far less cut and dried, however. Here the editor actually replies twice, once when you query and once when you submit the manuscript, after receiving a positive reply to the query.

There are three basic replies to a query: no response at all, no, or a go-ahead.

Waiting

Beginners panic if a personal letter isn't in their hands four days after the query has been mailed. ("Doesn't the editor know how important this is? How much time I spent to do it right?") Well, the truth of the matter is that you must give the editor two months to reply before you become concerned, unless it says even longer in *Writer's Market*. An editor can legitimately delay that long.

Also, the longer it's held, within reason, the more likely the response will be positive. Why? Because

it's probably being circulated to other editors involved in the approval process—and why circulate an
obvious rejection?

But if you haven't heard in two months, make a
copy of your copy of your original query letter. Attach
a letter or a note to that copy in which you say something to this effect: "The query letter attached was
sent to you on such-and-such a date. I'm enclosing a
copy in case the original was lost in the mail. Fortunately, the excitement of the idea it contains hasn't
diminished with age! Should we share it with your
readers? Please let me know at your earliest conve-
nience." Sign it, include an SASE, and send it off.

Waiting two months and then sending a copy of the
query letter with an explanatory message attached
seems far more sensible than doing what first comes
to mind: accusing the editor of being a shameless
s.o.b. or suggesting that he probably sold your idea to
some foreign rag for a royal ransom!

The reality is probably less dramatic. The query is
sitting on his desk with a question mark on it—
approve or not? Or the art director hasn't returned it.
Or it did get lost, more likely in the office mailroom
than the postal service. Or the editor likes it, but . . .
So what is needed is this gentle nudge by you. If your
query is on his desk, you will probably hear quickly.
If not, the editor will read the new query you just
sent—and respond to it.

After all, editors are remarkably like humans. They
even want to be treated with the same dignity as you.
A kindly reminder can't hurt; it might even prompt a
more thoughtful second reading of your query. But
wait the full two months. And don't burn any bridges
by railing at supposed slights. There aren't all that
many bridges for freelancers to burn!

If you still haven't heard after three months, send

your query to another publication. The original probably folded. Fortunately, it is quite rare for a reply to a query to take this long to arrive—or not arrive. Rejections usually come back first, frequently within 10 days of querying. Replies usually follow and are in your hands within two to three weeks. The chain of acceptance is usually longer than the chain of rejection.

Rejection

If you get a no, congratulate yourself on not having written the whole manuscript, unsolicited, and sending it to that editor. Your query saved you that time.

No writer is going to get a go-ahead from every query letter. Beginners might strike pay dirt about one out of six times. Even veterans at their selling best aren't likely to hit much better than one out of three to new markets. That means that in the best of conditions, for every three query letters you send out you can expect a positive reply from one. The maddening thing is that you can get five go-aheads in a row or a dozen consecutive rejections on a good idea. So you must write queries like salespeople going door to door: Give it your all each time and accept every turndown as one less rejection necessary to reach your selling average.

You can also learn from the kind of rejection you receive. If it's a standard, printed, impersonal form—unless the magazine has a huge circulation and receives thousands of queries a month—your query may not be getting top attention. On the other hand, if the editor writes a personal letter or note discussing your query and asking you to send more good ideas, that means your query was seriously considered. You want go-aheads, of course, but personal comments accompanying the rejections are strong, positive signs that you are close.

Why would an editor reject your query? Because the very idea you are proposing might already be set in type for one of the coming issues yet to appear on the stands. Or it might have crossed his desk a few months back, he sent a go-ahead to another free-lancer, and he's waiting to see that manuscript. Perhaps he has a bias against the subject, or it ran too recently on his pages, or he's certain that his readers aren't interested however well the piece is written. Or he has 14 super queries on his desk, including yours, with eight slots to fill. Some will be declined. The best of queries can strike out for solid reasons.

There's another reason that you might receive a no: You wrote a lousy query letter. In it you proved that however appealing the idea, you couldn't write it to that publication's level. Your query was muddled, flat, threatening; it was too aggressive, too groveling, too complex. In short, it didn't do what a query must. It didn't sell an idea and it didn't prove that you are the person to write about it for that magazine. The cure? Write better query letters!

Fortunately, rejection isn't fatal. All it says is "not now," "not here," "that idea just won't work for me," "I have too many other good ideas," "my pages are full for six months," "I just don't like it." There can be many reasons for a rejection, but the rejection in itself isn't personal unless you make the query personal.

If the first editor turns you down, query the next editor on your market list. If that editor says "no," try the third. Keep going until someone says yes, at which point you write it, sell it, and roll up the money wagon.

The first query letter does take time. You write it,

rework it, edit it, play around with it, and finally mail it. But the second query letter goes much faster. You take the best of the first, tempered by time, and mold it to meet another publication's needs. It's easier every time you do it. Writing the fifth query letter takes about as much time as a note to Cousin Luke.

Maybes and Yeses

So far we've been talking about negative or no replies. What happens if you get a table-thumping, rip-roaring yes? Don't count on it! Most go-aheads are quiet, qualified, tepid affairs. Something like "Let's see it," and little more.

The reason is buried in the term *contract* that we discussed earlier. Remember that of the three elements—offer, acceptance, and consideration— only acceptance stands between the query and a legal obligation. If the editor says "Yes, I will buy it," he must do just that, without regard to its final form or contents. So he is going to give you a qualified OK, a "let's see it" or "send it on spec" or "send the ms and let me decide." Which means you do the research, write the article in final form, and if it's what you promised, the chances are excellent it will be bought.

The other kind of positive response would be an assignment, a guarantee to buy what you produce or, through a "kill fee," at least pay a portion of the total amount if it proves unacceptable. Once you have been in print frequently on that editor's pages or at that level of publication, assignments become regular and expected.

But learners and even professionals in new markets generally write on speculation. You send a query to an editor who doesn't know you or your name. He isn't even sure that you wrote the query, though it bears your signature. So he wants to see how you write before making a full commitment.

Don't be discouraged by a conditional or speculative reply, however tepid. Respond to any clear encouragement with total vigor. Editors will say no unless they want to see your manuscript; they are simply too busy to tell you to send in material they won't consider seriously. So if the editor asks to see your article and you send what you promised at the level of writing needed, you have far better than a 50% chance of a sale.

Reading the Manuscript Replies

The next set of replies occurs after you have sent the query, received the go-ahead, prepared the manuscript, and mailed it to the editor for final approval. Here the editor can say yes, no, or some qualified in-between.

If it's yes, do something nice for yourself: Celebrate a victory worth winning. You are one printing away from being a famous writer! Now get going on another sale so you can tie down that toehold.

If it's a no, you probably lost the sale all on your own. There are two ways that's usually done. One has to do with the topic. You promised the editor one thing in the query but gave him something else in the article. You pitched the definitive piece about Chicago but along the way you became enraptured with Peoria. You said to yourself, if he likes Chicago he'll love Peoria, so you wrote the latter. The editor had Chicago written on his articles calendar so when the masterpiece about Peoria arrived, he rejected it without comment. He may agree that you did a super job on Peoria, but he was set on the Windy City, and you didn't deliver.

You can guess the other reason: The writing ranged from "not good enough" to just plain awful. This is the saddest of reasons, because if you can write a query good enough to get a go-ahead it's hard to imagine that, with enough attention to content and wording, you couldn't write an acceptable manuscript too.

There is a rare third response as well, or variety of responses. In summary, they are a one-chance opportunity to take a manuscript that is unusable as is and bring it up to acceptability. The editor indicates the shortcoming(s): It needs a new lead, better or more interviews, verification or validation of your facts, whatever. If the suggestions refer to the basic structure and should have been there from the outset, make the changes and consider yourself lucky to have a second chance.

What do you do with the finished article if the editor does turn you down? Should you forget it? Or maybe send it out unsolicited under a pseudonym?

None of the above. Sell it. Read the manuscript again, objectively, and see what of it and the original query would interest another editor. Something is worth saving since it already received one go-ahead.

If you switched subjects, as in our Chicago/Peoria example, then send your original query about the Chicago article to another market on your list. The query didn't get rejected, so modify it for a new editor and use it again. Just remember that if the second editor says yes, write about Chicago!

What do you do with that Peoria article? Write a super query that incorporates some of the better items in the article, and send it to likely markets, one at a time. (Don't mention that the article exists!) When an editor asks to see the article, read his publication, alter the already written piece to meet that magazine's

needs, and send it off. Not too fast, though. Give yourself a few weeks to "write" the masterpiece—again!

BIBLIOGRAPHY

Consult the current edition of the following publications:

Books

Burack, Sylvia, ed. *The Writer's Handbook.* The Writer.
Editor & Publisher International Yearbook.
Gale Directory of Publications.
Literary Market Place. R. R. Bowker.
Magazine Industry Market Place. R. R. Bowker.
Standard Periodical Directory. Oxbridge.
Ulrich's International Periodicals Directory. R. R. Bowker.
The Working Press of the Nation. National Research Bu-
reau.
Writer's Market. Writer's Digest Books.

Magazines

Publishers Weekly. R. R. Bowker.
The Writer.
Writer's Digest.

Newsletters

ASJA Newsletter, 1501 Broadway #1907, New York, NY
10036.
Travelwriter Marketletter, The Plaza Hotel #1745, New
York, NY 10019.
The Writer's Connection, 1601 Saratoga-Sunnyvale Road
#180, Cupertino, CA 95014.

Research Guides

Guide to Reference Books. American Library Association, 1980.
Reference Books: A Brief Guide. Enoch Pratt Free Library.
Todd, Alden. *Finding Facts Fast.* Ten Speed Press, 1979.

Form and Style

Buchman, Dian D., and Seli Grover. *The Writer's Digest Guide to Manuscript Formats.* Writer's Digest Books, 1987.
Chicago Manual of Style, 13th ed. University of Chicago Press, 1982.
Holley, Frederick. *The Los Angeles Times Stylebook.* New American Library, 1981.
Strunk, William Jr., and E. B. White. *The Elements of Style,* 3rd ed. Macmillan, 1979.
Zinsser, William. *Writing with a Word Processor.* Harper & Row, 1983.

Writing

Barzun, Jacques. *Simple and Direct: A Rhetoric for Writers,* rev. ed. Harper & Row, 1985.
Biagi, Shirley. *Interviews That Work.* Wadsworth, 1985.
Brady, John. *The Craft of Interviewing.* Writer's Digest Books, 1976.
Brohaugh, William, ed. *Just Open a Vein.* Writer's Digest Books, 1987.
Provost, Gary. *Make Every Word Count.* Writer's Digest Books, 1980.
Scott, Dewitt. *How to Write for People Who Think They Can't (And for People Who Think They Can).* Duncliff's International, 1985.
Tarshis, Barry. *How to Write Like a Pro.* NAL, 1982.
Venolia, Jan. *Rewrite Right!* Ten Speed Press, 1987.
Venolia, Jan. *Write Right!* Ten Speed Press, 1982.
Zinsser, William. *On Writing Well: An Informal Guide to Writing Nonfiction.* Harper & Row, 1985.

———■———

Every author, however modest, keeps a most outrageous vanity chained like a madman in the padded cell of his breast.

Logan Pearsall Smith, 1931

CHAPTER 9

Researching, Writing, and Mailing the Article

When your query gets a go-ahead, you have about three weeks to get the finished manuscript to the editor, unless the reply indicates another deadline or you made a different stipulation in your letter.

The latter is most likely for travel pieces where you query long in advance of the actual trip—as early as six months. Say you query in March about a trip in late May that will last two weeks. You will return about June 10, so add some three weeks to that and mention in your letter that the copy (and photography, if offered) will be in the editor's hands by July 1. You can indicate later dates for any manuscript, provided you have some reason for the delay.

There is nothing sacred about three weeks, but many editors feel that if they don't have the copy by that time, it will never arrive. So you might well adhere to that "deadline." It will force you to get working and will get copy to the editor while the subject is still relatively fresh.

Three weeks seems like three minutes to a beginner and three months to the pro. It's plenty of time, since you've decided on your article slant, know the publication the article will appear in, and have done the footwork in the feasibility study. What remains is the final research, the writing, and the mailing.

RESEARCHING

A few days of concentrated research should fill in the gaps left in your feasibility study, when you gathered facts, quotes, and anecdotes for the query and added them to your source list. To see what you need, and how to use it in the writing, you must now take those two or three recent articles in the publication you're writing for and subject them to all 12 steps in Figure 5, "How to Study a Printed Magazine Article."

The purpose at this point is to dissect examples of what the editor bought so you can produce an article utilizing the same or similar selling characteristics. (The more experienced you are at writing, the less necessary this tight modeling will be, but in the beginning it makes sense to let a winning article guide a new hand.) Short of having the editor instruct you, the best learning tool is an article the editor bought. Imitate it in quality, and to some degree form, and the chances are excellent that your article will also be bought.

You're looking for structure. Why are the articles set up as they are? Check for sentence length, the number of sentences per paragraph, the length of the lead and conclusion, and whether the pieces are written in first or third person. Who is quoted, and how many quotes per article will an editor tolerate? Is the copy funny, humorous, wry, catchy, dry, straight?

What question does the article answer? Is it asked in the lead? Is it asked at all? To find it, summarize the article in a sentence, turn that into a question, and voilà, the working question! Starting with it, what secondary questions came from the first to give the piece internal organization?

Set up your own outline. Take your working question and ask the secondary questions. Put them in an order: chronological, developmental, by region, whatever makes sense and is done in that publication. Then ask of each secondary question: Will the reader care? Is it important? The answers will determine whether that secondary question is retained, deleted, fattened, or barely mentioned.

How will you answer those questions, through fact, quote, or anecdote? How does that publication do it? And where will you find those three elements? Turn to your source list. Have you gathered enough material? Is it the best you can find? Is it current? Is it from the most reliable sources? Is it to the point and interesting?

Review the 12 steps again and apply them to your outline. Although you received a go-ahead, that just means "let me see it." Now you must produce the best copy possible. Complete the research begun at the feasibility stage. Add the new facts, set up your interviews, call for quotes, ferret out anecdotes. Writing is next.

WRITING

This segment will be shamefully short because, unfortunately, a book can't teach you how to write. (Nor is that this book's function: it is to show you how to sell your writing.) Even in person it would require getting into your skin and mind, then moving your hand. The best this tome can do is help you see how other selling writers write, share some observations, and point to a way that you can learn through key items in other articles.

Read an article each day about a topic that you want to write about in a magazine in which you want to appear. Do this for at least 10 days. Subject each of those articles to the 12 steps of "How to Study a Printed Magazine Article." Each article might take you an hour or more to do. It may be the best investment of time a learner can make.

You've already used the 12-step guide to extract sources and study article style for your query preparation. Now you will use it as a training tool, as the core of a regimen, to make you a selling writer by becoming an analytical reader.

By the time you finish the analytical reading of the 10 or more articles, you should know more than you would ever learn at "writing" classes or that this book could teach you. The system forces you to get inside the articles, to pull them apart, to rip the words from the bones, to see how ideas are organized and expressed in words that are chosen to appeal to the buying readers.

How could this book or 100 writing teachers tell you how to write for all of the thousands of publications needing your words? Let the writers in the latest issue of those publications show you what is being bought, then repeat what they did and take their place in the coming issues. It is a do-it-yourself learning procedure. When you learn it is up to you.

Having said that no book can teach you how to write, let's point a finger at some of the most important elements of copy that sell, so you know where to look for the hardest to learn: structure and manuscript mechanics.

Structure

Nothing is as important as the *lead* of an article. The first paragraph is what sells the editor and the reader. It pulls them into the piece and whets their appetite. Many call it the "hook" because it grabs the reader. Read the leads of the publications you want to sell to. Do they open with questions, examples, quotes, an offbeat fact, humor? What works for them?

Keep your leads to a sentence or two. They set the pace, inject the spirit, provide the pull that makes the reader want to read more. Study what is being used, then stick close to it in length and style.

You needn't write a lead first. Just start writing the story and worry about the lead later. Better yet, write many leads, 5 to 10 or more, before or after the rough body of the text is completed. Then select the best and bring the rest of the piece in line. Usually a few verb changes, some new transitions, and there you go.

A crucial element that is hard to describe, though easier seen, is the organizational or *transitional paragraph* which follows the lead. Generally it tells where the article is going and how it will get there. Leads often distort the direction of a piece by focusing on one aspect of it or by grabbing for the reader's attention with word play. Thus it is left to the second (and sometimes third and even fourth) paragraph(s) to straighten out the theme, set up the process of discussing it, and establish the true tone.

The transitional paragraph most often tells the method of discussion. It indicates that the topic will be presented chronologically, by city, by steps of development, etc. It is also called the "bridge," because it links the lead to the body through the use of conjunctive thoughts. Without a well-designed transitional paragraph many, perhaps most, articles would make little sense. So study them closely. They can be the difference between selling success and a lot of words going nowhere.

New writers are surprised at the brevity of leads until they look at the *length of paragraphs*. Most of your paragraphs should be the same length as the lead: a sentence or two long, sometimes three but almost never four. Large blocks of copy are avoided in articles because they impede reading flow and intimidate the reader. Favor the newspaper approach: two sentences maximum. (Impossible? Find a newspaper and start counting!)

Books, incidentally, have longer paragraphs!

Study the magazines. Their needs are different from school essays, which most new writers use as models of form. In school one wrote paragraphs until the subject or the writer expired. Not so in commercial writing. After a couple of sentences (or roughly six typed lines), it's time for a new paragraph. Write for speed and clarity. Break the material up with quotes or anecdotes. Keep your descriptions tight and short, if needed at all. Verify this by reading.

The *conclusion* is also important. Articles aren't O. Henry stories with surprise or trick endings. News pieces simply run out when they end. Most articles differ from this in that their conclusions must reinforce what their leads promise. If it's a patriotic piece, the conclusion should make you want to stand up and salute. If nostalgia is its theme, you should have a lump in your throat when you read the last word. You get the idea, but let's share another old writer's trick, because some articles almost defy satisfactory conclusion.

If you are having trouble finding a tight, clear, reinforcing ending, look for a word or a phrase from the lead that can be comfortably repeated in the final paragraph. You've seen this a hundred times and probably never paid any attention to it. Now it will jump out at you every time it's done! Repeating an item from the beginning of the article at the conclusion creates the sense of having gone full circle, of a journey completed. Just don't force it. (Beware of reusing something from the title, however. Since titles are often changed entirely, a reference in the conclusion to a defunct title won't make much sense.)

Speaking of *titles*, in newspapers your title may never be used, since they must be set in headline form. But in other selling markets, think of a title as the first lead, though only a few words long, that will make the reader want to see more of what you have written. The title pulls the reader to the actual lead, which continues that pull into the body. Once there, studies show, the reader will finish the article if it sustains interest and doesn't have a large copy block that obstructs easy comprehension.

A good title tells what the article is about. In humor it must reflect the same level of humor as the piece itself. If the article is dry and wry, a twist of the same is called for in the title. If it's a side-holder, the title had better be funny. Editors rarely change humor titles, so attention is vital there. The best humor titles, incidentally, come from the heart of the material—never the lead—and therefore are written last. Finish the article, write a dozen titles, and try them on your friends. Ask them what they think the article is about. No inside jokes in the title, though.

These are the most important elements of copy that sells. No two articles are the same. Read analytically what is being bought, then write more of it—better.

Manuscript Mechanics

It's one thing to have the right words and use them in the right way. It's another to present the final manuscript to the editor in a properly salable package.

Between writing and form, writing is many times more important. Yet there are certain things that will get your query rejected fast, like sending it handwritten or in a language not quite English. And other things that make editors' lives hard, and hence yours less rewarded. So let's highlight those things, talk a bit about why you want your submission to look good, and offer some general guidelines about a manuscript form that seems to be widely acceptable.

Still, super writing is hard for any editor to reject. As the *Writer's Market* write-up for the Sunday magazine of the *Providence Journal* used to say, after offering the standard submission advice, "But if your stuff is really good, we'll buy it if it comes in by pony express."

The magic words are "really good." The piece must be super to overcome lousy packaging and marketing. Bring the packaging and marketing up to standard and any copy has a far better chance of being bought. That's particularly important for beginners whose first copy is more likely "good" than "really good." Poor presentation of a good idea is a liability you can't afford.

Then too, you are posing as a professional while you grow into the suit. Make the pose believable by doing what professionals do: Offer clean copy, on-time delivery, names and labels where they should be, and so on. (The reality is that some professionals are slobs, just like some beginners, and God knows how they hurdled the barrier but they did. They break every rule, even where no true rules exist, and con-

Figure 11 First Page of a Queried Manuscript

1900 words

THE LAND OF THE MUSIC MAN

by Gordon Lee Burgett

River City, U.S.A., is alive and hiding in north-central
Iowa, much as Harold Hill described it to the nation in Meredith Willson's 1957 smash hit, *The Music Man.*

"Ya got trouble, friend,
Right here, I say,
Trouble right here in River City!"

The trouble, you recall, was a billiards hall called the
Pleazol, and the cure was a marching band—instruments to
be bought, sight unseen, from one Harold Hill.

If you too laughed and applauded the author's foot-
tapping imagination, then wend your way to Mason City,
Iowa, walk north on the west side of Federal Avenue from
Central Park, and look down. There tiled in the pavement
for all to see: PLEAZOL! (Trouble lurks a few doors away
where billiards continue to "threaten" the morals of the local youth.)

Gordon Lee Burgett
1234 Fifth St.
Santa Maria, CA 93456

tinue to sell well and often. But they are in the wee minority, tolerated but not loved. Emulate them, if you must, after you've sold your 500th article.)

Now for some guidelines, using Figure 11 as an example. When you are preparing your final manuscript, type on standard size (8½ x 11") white paper, one side only. Use a typewriter with elite or pica type, not script. The ribbon should be reasonably new and black. Clean the keys if they are clogged up with ink—the "c," "e," and "o" should be clear and are good cleaning guides. If you're using a word processor, avoid dot matrix, although some can be double-struck to look almost identical to "regular" type and may be acceptable.

Don't run your words from one edge of the page to the other. Fifteen spaces for the left margin is enough for the editor to write in typesetting instructions; leave about the same space on the unjustified right side.

Start the copy halfway down your first page. At the top of that page write the title in capital letters. Don't underline it or put quotation marks around it unless they are needed to indicate a nickname or other special designation. Center the title in the middle of the top half of page 1. About three lines below it, also centered, type "by" followed by your name. (That is your "by-line.") In the upper right corner write the approximate word count, rounded off to the closest 25. You can handwrite the number in after the manuscript is completely typed, then counted. (Each word counts. Even little words.)

Indent each paragraph five spaces, double-space between the lines (you can triple-space between paragraphs if you wish), and leave a lot of white space at the bottom. If you want the typesetter to leave white between sections of your copy, skip about five lines and type the space symbol—#—in the center of that white opening. Don't suffocate your editor with too much copy per page; surround the copy with plenty of blank paper.

Don't leave "widows," short lines at the bottom or top of a page. They bedevil editors because typesetters frequently miss them and turn your copy into senseless babble. Newspaper editors particularly dislike them—and many magazine editors started with newspapers.

If you want to indicate italics in your copy, don't type it with an italic font. All italics should be *underlined*. If you want bold face, type it regular, underline it with a wavy line, and write B.F. in large letters in the left margin in line with the words you want set that way.

Put your name and address on every page. A quick way is to use the 1,000-for-a-dollar return address stickers in the lower right corner.

At the top of each inside page, about six lines down from the top and six lines above the copy, flush left in line with the margin, write the title or an abbreviated form in capital letters, your name in lowercase, and the page number. For example: MUSIC MAN, Burgett, 3.

On the last page of copy, a few lines below the last words, center the word END, or type -30- (a printer's symbol meaning there is nothing more to typeset), or ####.

Onionskin paper makes editors weep: it curls up and turns yellow. Likewise, avoid erasable paper. The minute a thumb touches the typing, the words are lost. Plain white paper, 20-pound or mimeo, is fine. The idea is that the copy is permanent, legible, and flat.

Two punctuation problems plague new writers.

One, semicolons; use them rarely, but correctly. A high school primer will explain how. Second, learn how to use dashes. A dash on your typewriter is two hyphens. Never end a typed manuscript line with a hyphen, even if it looks odd to carry the whole word to the next line. Carry it over, with the typesetter's blessing.

Those are the usual needs and problems. Common sense and editors' eyesight rule. Remember, if the copy is super, it can even arrive by pony express.

MAILING

Mailing the article! What a relief!

You want your manuscript to arrive as quickly as possible, flat, intact, and undamaged. And you want to receive a response with the same positive haste. For the latter you must include an SASE large enough to contain your manuscript plus a reply letter or note. Most editors will return your material even if you don't send an SASE, despite their threats, but they don't like it, do it v e r y, v e r y s l o w l y, and may decide not to give you a positive reply because you look so much like an amateur by not sending the SASE.

SASEs should be the same size (if you want the manuscript back) as the original envelope, folded in half with the stamps already affixed. If you don't want the manuscript back, as may be the case with si-multaneous submissions, a small stamped envelope should be included that is large enough to hold a reply.

If you send items abroad, or even to Canada, you should include an international reply coupon (IRC) with a self-addressed envelope so the receiving editor needn't pay to reply.

You should paper-clip (not staple) all magazine and newspaper manuscripts and send book manuscripts unclipped. No report covers or binders.

Cover letters must be sent with simultaneous submissions, of course, as we explained in Chapter 7. They may be necessary for single submissions that are not preceded by a query, like fillers or humor, but only if you have something to say: your writing background, special expertise in the subject, and so on. Just that you want the editor to buy isn't enough. He knows.

Rarely do you need a cover letter for queried articles or books, unless there is something special in the contents or that has occurred since the query that affects the manuscript. Don't try to sell at that point. Let the copy do the work.

The outside wrapping should be sturdy enough to protect the work against rough handling in transit. It should be tightly sealed and include both your return address and the name of a person, with address, where it is being sent. If you don't know the proper name, you can send it to the appropriate editor: Articles Editor, Managing Editor, etc. If the piece is six pages or fewer, you can fold it like a regular letter and sent it in a business envelope. Anything larger should be sent flat.

A book manuscript sent unbound in a box should include a return address tag and sufficient stamps for its return paper-clipped to the top of the manuscript. Book publishers rarely use the same box and never the same wrapping.

There are less expensive ways to ship or mail, but first class is the best. The item arrives in a few days, will be returned if the publication folded while you were gathering the facts and words, and gets far less mauling. Write FIRST CLASS in giant letters on the wrapping so it gets sent that way. Forget insurance: It pays only the cost of the paper and typing if collected. Just keep a copy of everything you mail, and should it go astray—it almost never happens, despite the usual grumbling about the postal service—you can mail another copy.

Most editors feel that certified or registered mail isn't worth the expense. Some resent it, thinking that it signals trouble ahead, that the writer thinks the editor will steal the work and never pay so the signature of receipt will serve for later litigation. Alas, it is usually signed for, if at all, by the mail clerk!

To mail photos, pack large prints inside cardboard inserts and write on the envelope in large letters: "PHOTOS—DO NOT BEND." Put a rubber band around the inserts and include your manuscript in the same envelope. Send it first class, of course.

Slides are less risky to mail because of the sturdy acetate holders with 20 slots into which one slide each can be inserted. Put these sheets between cardboard inserts and it would take determination to damage them. No glass mounts!

Every print or slide must be identified. Stamp or print your name on the back of each print or proof sheet; the 1,000-for-a-dollar stickers are again ideal since they adhere well. They also hold securely on paper-mounted slides, or you can write your name and address on each slide. Write captions to explain what each photo is about. Number them to correspond with your prints or slides. Mark each caption or sheet with your name and address.

Photos or slides are sent only when requested by the editor. They do not accompany query letters or simultaneous submissions, but are offered at that phase of the transaction. If the photos or slides are valuable, make copies and keep at least one of each valuable item.

How do you keep track of the query letters, simultaneous submissions, photos, slides, and all the details that come from mailing and the resulting responses? A simple mailing record, like the one in Figure 12, will help maintain your sanity, provide a valuable record for the IRS, and keep you on schedule.

The mailing record is kept on plain 8½ x 11" paper, with the year and most recent page number on top and about an inch and a half between the six or so entries per page so you have room for notations where needed. Record every item, query, or submission when it is mailed, and likewise note all incoming mail about those items in the entry.

Not only will the mailing record prevent you from sending the same query or manuscript to the same editor more than once, it serves as proof of volume of work for an IRS audit, reminds you which editors have not replied, which are prompt and buy often, and how much income you are earning from your writing.

The top section of the sample mailing record shows five queries and one simultaneous submission manuscript, each listed at the time of mailing. It is based on a topic-spoking (see Chapter 11) of the Mason City/ River City idea that was never done and thus is fictitious, although two of the bottom entries actually did appear in print. Copies of those articles appear in Appendices A and B.

The bottom section uses a system I devised over the years to keep a quick visual tally of the stages of each entry. Let's go through the items to explain their sta-

Figure 12 Sample Mailing Record

MAILING RECORD

1/17	Q - History: Mason City, 1912	**Des Moines Sunday Register Picture Magazine**
1/17	Q - Cement/Mason City	**Constructor Magazine**
1/18	Q - Clear Lake/Mason City	**Gray's Sporting Journal**
1/18	Q - Music/Mason City, 1912	**Music Magazine**
1/19	Q - Land of Music Man	**Travel Magazine**
1/19	Music Man (news travel)	**Washington Post**

(above list one month later)

1/17 Q - History: Mason City, 1912   **Des Moines Sunday Register Picture Magazine**

1/17 Q - Cement/Mason City   **Construction Magazine**

1/18 Q - Clear Lake/Mason City   **Gray's Sporting Journal**
1/29 - OK, spec 3000 wds, $500-1000 pub. + pix
2/14 - sent ms/40 slides

1/18 Q - Music/Mason City, 1912   **Music Magazine**
1/23 - send right away, have hole: 2000 wds, $150 + pix, $15-100
1/27 - send ms/35 b/w's and 30 slides
2/13 - bought ms, 2 b/w's, 2 slides
2/17 - paid ($400)

1/19 Q - Land of Music Man   **Travel Magazine**
2/2 - looks good for June issue/$300 +/–

1/19 Music Man (news travel)   **Washington Post**
2/6 - holding for possible spring use,
no pix requested/maybe $100

---

tus on the day we see this list, which would be 2/19, one month after the last item was entered.

1. The history query to the *Des Moines Sunday Register* supplement was rejected. With a red felt pen I simply cross out the rejections, so if

necessary I can read through the red to see where it was sent. I would query another history publication on that market list the day I received that rejection, or quickly thereafter.

2. The construction magazine seems to be moving with the haste of cement. It has actually been only a month, though, and it makes no sense to get excited for at least two months, so this entry is unmarked. If it is still unmarked on 3/17, I'll send a copy of the same query with a note attached suggesting that the original probably got lost in the mail. Is the idea right for the pages of their trade publication?

3. *Gray's Sporting Journal*, let's say, responded nine days later, eager to see a 3,000-word piece on spec, with b/w's and/or slides. I note that, plus the pay range from *Writer's Market*, as well as the bad news that they pay on publication. On the other hand, if there's another hand, they pay very well. When I mail the manuscript and slides I record that. The brackets mean I received a positive reply and the item is in process.

4. As unlikely as this entry is, with its extremely tight time frame, I wanted to show an item queried, sent, and paid for. Which is what the box indicates: accepted for publication. The money in the circle means the actual amount received! You can follow the progress of this query and submission. What makes it worth the hustle is the money paid for the photos and slides.

5. We follow the *Travel* magazine example step by step in Chapter 13, but this is what it looks like at the early stages on the mailing list: a query

and a tepid go-ahead. The go-ahead gets the brackets drawn, as would any positive reply. If they buy it, it gets boxed; if it's rejected, crossed out in red. Several weeks after the nod, I sent the manuscript and photos. The rest is history.

6. To show a simultaneous submission I moved up the true date of the *Washington Post's* actual mailing—in reality it followed the *Travel* piece by several months, in the early summer when folks might be Iowa-bound. The list would also show a dozen or so entries to other newspaper travel editors on the same date, each to be filled in when the editors reject or hold/accept the articles. Since newspaper travel pays on publication, and that can delay for months, this will sit unbracketed or unboxed until I receive the good news, usually with a copy of the issue page with that item in print.

Finally, a few words in defense of mailing in general. If you don't, you will never sell. Anyway, the worst the editor can say is no. Those no's are the fertilizer from which yeses grow. So bolster your courage and get your words in the mail. Do something to reward yourself while you await the verdict. If you are gutsy enough to take on the writing world and bright enough to do it right, surely you can figure out how to honor yourself for being a winner!

QUESTIONS, ANSWERS, AND ADDITIONAL THOUGHTS

Q: What are tear sheets and stringers?

A: "Tear sheets" is an antiquated term straight out of the *Front Page* era. When freelancers were published they were given the page on which their work appeared, torn out of the newspaper. They were paid by the inch at the end of the week. The word "stringer" appeared because the inches were measured with a string. The writer pasted his copy from the tear sheets in one-column width, then used a string to indicate the linear inches. The string was held up to a yardstick to see how much he should be paid. A tear sheet now means a copy, and a stringer is a freelancer, generally living distant from the city of publication, who contributes occasional pieces to a magazine or newspaper. If something occurs in their town or area, stringers are contacted to write it up.

Q: Writing with a colleague?

A: Disaster looms. Sagging-fleshed professionals with years in the trade shudder at the thought. It can't be any easier for beginners.

On the surface it looks easy: One does the research, the other writes, or some similar division of labor. Yet the reality is so seldom like the ideal that the number of successful collaborators in freelance writing is pitifully small, and those are almost always in book writing, usually texts.

My advice? Learn your trade alone. That's demanding enough without having to wrestle with another's personality and erratic schedule. When you can do it yourself, find another of like ability, if you insist on coauthoring. By then most see the folly of the thought.

Q: Three weeks? You've got to be kidding!

A: What do you do if you can't have the manuscript in the editor's hands in three weeks? If it will be just a few days late, do nothing. No apologies needed, unless the editor specifically set a deadline and you will miss it. But if you will be many days late, tell the editor when you know—and why. "I'm busy" or "The typewriter needs cleaning" are not the kind of reasons editors accept. "I've just unearthed some super news we have to include" or "The key interview was delayed because . . . and it will be rescheduled on . . ." are more forgivable. Then give the editor a new, firm date and stick to it. You get about one delay per editor—the first sale is the worst time to use it. Incidentally, don't believe what you see in the movies about writers always being late. Some are, of course: big names and ex-writers. The big names got that way because they weren't late in the beginning.

———————■———————

> Clear writers, like fountains, do not seem so
> deep as they are; the turbid look the most
> profound.
>
> Walter Savage Landor,
> 1755-1864

PART THREE

Multiplying
the Sales

CHAPTER 10

Reselling the Sales

O nce your article has been in print, why not sell it again and again? Or use the same research and rewrite it for other publications? It's commonly done, perfectly legal, and can increase your income remarkably.

If your article appeared in a magazine, say, you can use the same material in newspapers or a book. And if the original publication circulates only in North America, why should the rest of the world be deprived of your rapier wit and literary charm?

Professional writers seldom have to be convinced of the wisdom of these practices. They want to know how each can be done—so none of the extra sales are lost!

REPRINTS

Reprints are second-rights sales. (The terms "reprint rights" and "second rights" are identical.) They almost always mean that a publication bought your article on a first-rights basis, it was printed, and you subsequently sold it to another publication.

You can sell those rights again the minute a first-rights sale hits the stands. You needn't ask the editor who bought the first rights for permission or a release. He used what he bought. First rights means "one-time (first) use," with those rights automatically reverting to you when used.

There is no exclusivity to second or reprint rights. They are simply a reprinting by anyone at any time, with your approval and their payment, of an item that's already been in print. (There are no third or fourth rights.) You needn't change a word in the original and you can offer it simultaneously to any publication you think will buy it.

When you offer second or reprint rights you must tell the potential buyer (1) where the piece first appeared in print, (2) the date of that appearance, and (3) that you are offering second or reprint rights.

One way to hawk seconds is to cut and paste the published version of the article and make clear copies of it. Send a copy to each possible buyer with a cover letter or note. You can even offer the same piece to competing publications. But if both buy and use them, though they should have known that there was no exclusivity, they'll both be mad at you, which could close both markets to future sales.

As explained in Chapter 7, begin this cover letter, like the one in Figure 13, with some lively paragraphs telling what the manuscript attached is all about. The letter is a tease to get the editor to read the actual piece, so do it up right—how many will read the paste-up unless the letter makes it sound irresistible? Then include items (1)–(3) above. If you have additional material that would enhance the sale, such as photos or sidebars, mention it next. Finally, offer to send the original, double-spaced manuscript to facilitate typesetting. (If they are interested, they

Figure 13 Sample Reprint Cover Letter

1234 Fifth St.
Santa Maria, CA 93456
(805) 555-5555
September 3, 1974

Mr. Sempre Compra
Editor, Reprint Magazine
3456 Pulaski Ave.
Chicago, IL 60611

Dear Mr. Compra:

How many of your readers have succumbed to the goose bump epidemic affecting 20 million Americans—caused by 76 trombones?

Those same trombones that cause hand-clapping, foot-tapping, and yesteryear-longing as your readers return to an oompahpahing Iowa town in 1912, River City, U.S.A., every time they see Meredith Willson's The Music Man?

A cure can grace your pages! A fun, fact-filled look at the real River City! An upbeat article that transports your actual and armchair travelers to Mason City, Iowa, where Willson was born, spent 1912 as a 10-year-old boy in the school band, left to join Sousa and Toscanini, and returned regularly to lead the trombones—though not the same sold by that fictitious Harold Hill—to the rousing finale of his musical.

The article, attached as it appeared on a first-rights basis in Travel magazine in July 1974, is now available to you as a reprint. I can also provide an assortment of b/w horizontals and verticals plus some forty 35mm slides for your selection, on a one-time rights basis, if interested.

To update the piece I can also add a sidebar about activities and events that will take place in that area—if you would give me an approximate date when the piece would be read, the lead time required, and length stipulations for the box.

Finally, to facilitate typesetting I have the article in original manuscript form, if you plan to use it. Let me know if interested.

As for me, I've been in print some 400 times now in maga-

> zines, mostly in travel, humor, and general interest. But the
> enclosed article tells all. It must be read to be loved—or to
> spread its beneficent curative powers. By your readers as
> well as yourself! Should we share the balm?
>
> Gordon Burgett

will probably want the manuscript version. Since
most of the users will pay on publication, this helps
you locate those who are most interested so you can
make sure that the actual users pay.) Don't forget to
include an SASE.

REWRITES

Rewrites are what they say: the original article rewritten. They have their own identity. They are new, different articles that can be sold like any other article:
all rights, first rights, as simultaneous submissions,
and so on.

A rewrite will likely use some or all of the research
material used for the original. But it will do so in such
a way that the resulting article will have an identity
of its own.

An article might talk about the Chicago Cubs since
1876, when the National League began and that team
won the first pennant. A rewrite might talk about
1876 only, that team, and that pennant. A different rewrite might focus on Anson, Spaulding, and the lumi-
naries of that year; another might discuss the greatest
Cubs from 1876 to the present.

When are rewrites most commonly done? When
you have sold all rights to an article and you want to
spin off more sales from the piece and its research.
Since an editor buying all rights has bought only the

copy, not the idea, you can reuse the idea in different ways, as well as any additional information about it, for as long as that topic generates sales.

The question of how much one article must differ from another to have its own legal identity is hard to answer. Surely if you change the title, lead, conclusion, and quotes, that ought to be difference enough. Another approach is easier, though: changing the angle. Come at the topic from a different tack. That will require a new title. The old lead won't work, and since the conclusion is intimately linked to the lead, it too must change. You could even use some of the old quotes, since they refer to a different base.

Modified Reprints

Unlike the standard "reuse-it-as-it-is" reprint, some reprints require some rewriting to make the piece acceptable.

Let's continue our baseball example, slightly altered. Say it's early 1991 and you write an article about "The National League Since 1876," taking advantage of the 115th anniversary to write a funny, fact-filled article about the heroics and foibles of that organization. You sell it as a simultaneous submission to the weekly newspaper supplements (and to a few sports editors at papers with no supplements). So far no problems. If everybody buys the same manuscript, bingo!

Alas, nothing is perfect. Cincinnati, let's say, lauds the article but says it needs a stronger local orientation. Read: modified reprint. More material about the Reds of now and yesteryear must be woven into the basic article the others bought. You have 80% of the research completed and copy written, with 20% to add, mostly from sources you've already used. Is it worth the extra time and effort to custom-wrap a general piece for a particular editor?

That's your decision, but if the pay is worth the additional hassle, modified reprints can be a lucrative, efficient path to salvaging otherwise lost sales.

You might even offer modifications when you pursue resales. If you write an article that you suspect is close to an editor's interests but not quite usable as is, suggest in your cover letter with the paste-up of the original printed article that you would gladly provide the material "as is or with modifications you suggest." The ideal is to sell reprints as they are, to try to get as much mileage out of a sold manuscript as possible. Better than no sales, though, is selling reprints altered to fit a different readership's needs.

A modified reprint, if sufficiently altered to create a distinct piece, has all the virtues of a rewrite. There's no reason it can't be sold to the publication on a first-rights or lesser basis, then resold later as a reprint once it has appeared in print. It's a reprint of a rewrite, really. Remember, a rewrite is a new manuscript with its own rights. Even it can have reprints!

MIXED MARKETS

The question here is whether you can reuse an item in other markets or media. The answer is an unqualified yes/no. It depends on how it was sold and how receptive the other media are to used material.

Looking first at different markets within the printed-word area, we find much of what we must say has been said before. If you sell an article all rights, you can't use it later in a book, newsletter, or anywhere else as is without begging those rights back. If you sell it first rights, you can, without begging.

Along the same line, you can sell simultaneous submissions to newspaper travel, regional magazines, and in-flights as long as each knows and there is no significant readership overlap. The simplest example might be a piece sold to newspapers in the West, regionals in the Southeast, and in-flights in the Northeast. Or you could sell a first-rights piece to a national magazine, rewrite it for another, sell reprints from both anywhere, and still work that topic into an all-rights article, if clearly unique, for some metropolitan high-roller.

As for mixing the media, it's rare that an item prepared for print will fit in, without modifications, elsewhere. Articles don't serve as TV documentary scripts, for example, without massive alterations. Since you are selling a way to express an idea in copy, not the idea itself, the alterations so change that mode of expression that the rights issue becomes moot. And so it is with almost any example you can conjure up. Rework the idea into proper form for the new medium and you must by necessity leave the old form behind. This might seem unduly simplistic, but the guideline is valid. If you feel that it doesn't apply to your unusual case, ask the person to whom you are attempting to resell your article.

SALES ABROAD

Think of the billions who are not getting to read the masterpiece about the Chicago Cubs or "Three-Finger" Mordecai Brown that you have grand-slammed across the U.S.

Why are you depriving the rest of the world of that prose? If you sold it all rights, we know. You need to do a rewrite. But if you sold anything less, you probably have most of the globe as virgin territory.

Writer's Market indicates the rights purchased. Usually those rights are limited geographically: U.S., North American, etc. What falls outside that designation is yours, and if you can find a way to convert your English into the many tongues that others speak, read, and write, plus find publications willing to pay you to share your article with their readers, you have many resales still unrealized.

Unless you know specific foreign markets and are truly fluent in their tongue (or they will handle the translation), however, don't bother mailing manuscripts abroad to other than English-language publications. Canada would be the most obvious market but is usually covered in original purchases since most buy North American rights. Check, of course. The Australian market is also particularly receptive to U.S. writers and topics.

Syndicates

The most practical way to sell to the rest of the world is through syndicates that sell abroad. Check that classification in *Writer's Market*. You sell your manuscripts to them precisely the same way you sell to U.S. magazine editors: Query the person buying material for the syndicate and convince him that what you have for sale will interest his foreign readers. If the material has been in print, explain which rights were originally bought. If not, explain which rights you are offering for sale. (Normally you do not dicker over rights in a query letter. If rights are discussed, it would be after you have a go-ahead. But in this case it is clearly a key element to the sale. You may indicate, for example, that you are offering "all rights outside North America.")

Include all you have available for the syndicate's consideration. If it's one unpublished article, include the manuscript with a query that helps sell it. If you have three articles, one unpublished and two up for resales, send the unpublished manuscript plus a paste-up of each of the printed pieces, with a query, two pages maximum (one preferred), written to accommodate this odd assortment. Explain the rights available for each. Indicate photos or slides you can provide, and offer to send them for the editor's consideration.

If the syndicate is interested, it will take one or all of your articles. It will want to see your slides or your photos, to be reproduced. It will translate your material into other tongues, offer your piece(s) to other markets, and probably pay you about half of what it makes on everything sold. Payment schedules vary but are often at set intervals (quarterly, every four months, etc.). Finally, most syndicates will send you copies of your articles in languages that will amuse your kin and convince you that your talent is truly universal.

Selling abroad is slow, rather low-paying, and remote from your control, but the money floating in unheralded is truly lovely. And why not? If you can have them rolling in the aisles in Keokuk or nodding with admiration in Albany, why should the souls of Ankara or Inhambupe be deprived?

QUESTIONS, ANSWERS, AND ADDITIONAL THOUGHTS

Q: Reprints for simultaneous submissions?

A: The first and second rights of simultaneous submissions can be confusing. Simultaneous sales presume separate spheres of readership to which the piece is being sold for a "first" viewing. An article to the travel sections of the *Chicago Tribune, Los Angeles Times,* and *Boston Globe,* for example, is bought by each on the assumption that its readers will see it first on its pages. You can sell it simultaneously as widely as possible to as many nonoverlapping publication readerships as you can identify. You could then sell it as a reprint nationwide as soon as it has been published in each market where it was accepted or held for later use.

Time and overlap are your problems here. One buyer might print your article in a week, another in a year. It makes much more sense to rewrite simultaneous submission pieces from a fresh angle and free yourself of having to keep track of publication dates and circulation boundaries. Rewrites have their own life and can be sold at the same time as simultaneous sales, later, to the same readers, or to anybody—just so the copy is significantly different.

Q: **Raise your income $50–$100 on most sales?**

A: Add sidebars or boxes to your main copy, which should up the ante this much, often more. *Time* magazine uses boxes all the time. A major piece about, say, the war in the Near East will be accompanied by a box that will either focus on the theme from a larger view—comparing the current impasse with historical parallels or putting it into world perspective—or concentate on a minute element, like kids attending school amidst shelling at a borderline kibbutz or the warm family life of a key leader.

If you're writing about attending the World Series, the box might tell where visitors can park. An article about improvements in running shoes might have a sidebar with details about the newest models. If you write about whale watching, a box will tell where you can make reservations to see the spouting behemoths. You get the idea.

————■————

Write without pay until somebody offers to pay.
If nobody offers within three years, the
candidate may look upon this circumstance
with the most implicit confidence as a sign that
sawing wood is what he was intended for.

Mark Twain, 1835-1910

CHAPTER 11

Converting the Process into Big Money

A long time back we spoke of a losing formula practiced by most beginners: take one idea, write one article, and submit one manuscript directly to a magazine for purchase and print. A loser because you must complete all the research and writing without knowing beforehand whether the item is wanted, needed, or will even be considered.

But there's another formula that's a loser in the long run. Take one idea, send a query, receive a positive reply, write a manuscript, sell it, and do the same thing again . . . and again . . . and again. Yes, precisely what this book has been urging you to do up to now—and showing you how!

The problem isn't the process. It's the scope.

If you *really* want to make money by writing, follow that process but add a major new element at the beginning that will multiply your research yield, expedite your querying and preparation, and put the maximum number of manuscripts in print in the least amount of time.

TOPIC-SPOKING

For want of a better name let's call it topic-spoking, and explain how it differs from what we have been advocating. In topic-spoking you take a solid idea or topic and, rather than extract one article from it, use it as the core of many related articles, all drawing from an extended feasibility study done to create a reference/resource pool and knowledge bank. The name comes from the spokelike appearance of the article ideas radiating from a central hub of shared knowledge, as Figure 14 shows.

The concept is more readily grasped through example, so this chapter will follow a huge one—whales—pursued to greater depth, appropriately.

Topic-spoking requires a deviation in timing and an expansion of risk over the standard query-write-sell-resell/rewrite process. In both, the subject is expanded from one article idea to 6, 10, 20, or as many as energy and the readers' interest dictates. (This example is limited to 8 because of space limitations.)

As one idea is investigated before querying, so are the rest. The wider the research expands, the more article ideas (represented by spokes) emerge. Some, later, will fade for want of sufficient information or markets.

The long-term savings is in time. It is easier and faster to extract possible articles, and gather basic querying information, about many subjects with the same base than it is to return to that material each time you want to explore another of the many related ideas. It saves time, as well, in the long run, to compile one extended source list, of items in print about the subject and of authorities to interview, spending a few extra hours to form a solid working bibliography from which information touching many related ideas can be drawn, than to create or add to a basic list each time you return to the library.

The risk is that you may spend too much pre-query time developing a topic-spoking program and process than is justified by later sales. Yet with far greater rewards come greater risks. In the balance, with good ideas and sales diligently pursued, the rewards here far outweigh those risks.

Finally, since query letters contain but a few paragraphs of hard facts, quotes, or anecdotes, it is simply easier to gather up some pages of each to sprinkle, as they apply, through many queries about the same general subject, selecting from the information pool those morsels that match or enhance the promise each query makes.

Soon we will wallow with whales, but first it is important that you understand why topic-spoking is superior to the "one-idea, one-sale" system and when it can be used.

With the one-idea, one-sale approach you spend a considerable amount of time at the feasibility, query, and research-writing stages just to receive a few hundred dollars from a sale. Even with reprints and rewrites, the per-hour earnings ratio makes freelance article writing a highly skilled, low-paying discipline. And good material unearthed by research is often quickly abandoned in the quest for another idea/query/sale.

Admittedly, that's painting the picture one-dimensionally. One supposes that most professionals, as they become familiar with the selling process, opt to use the same research more than once, if for no other reason than it is there and easier to use than digging elsewhere, again. Beginners, on the other hand, are usually afraid to reuse the same information. They think that used ideas or rehashed facts are somehow wrapped in law or copyright and they fear a suit if they mention the same thing, even in different words, in more than one manuscript. So they avoid topic-spoking, or anything similar, through timidity or ignorance.

This chapter suggests that topic-spoking is not only permissible, it may be the best of all paths to fiscal comfort through the thicket of serial selling. To state it even more strongly, topic-spoking should be the first new term in your planning vocabulary the minute you start selling your writing. Once you've made $100 or $325 or $500 from an early single sale, find the strongest idea in your bag, topic-spoke it, and strive for a minimum of $1,000, $2,000, or much more per idea.

Does it sound absurd, particularly if your hand shakes and your head reels at the thought of querying your first piece? It may be asking too much of the true greenhorn. If you are new to the field, concentrate 100% on making that first sale, then on selling reprints and rewrites. Learn every facet of the process. But then go back and topic-spoke that first idea or another equally as strong. Branch out, expand that research, move into related subtopics and to new publications. Use a good first-sale experience as the hub of your first topic-spoking, then apply again and again the same steps you already took to make that first sale, but on a faster, more efficient base.

Fortunately, topic-spoking can be done after the initial sale has been made, though it makes most sense when done at the feasibility phase. So if you have been selling only one article per idea, you can return, pick the best ideas, and topic-spoke to gather up lost sales.

A Whale of an Example

At last, how to expand a big idea from the beginning into far bigger sales.

The idea is whales. A common enough sight from the shore of southern California where the grays, the oldest existing cetaceans, pass close to land on their annual roundtrip from the Arctic to Baja California. There they mate, give birth, and fatten up for the longest known mammal migration. By the one-idea, one-sale system you are limited to one topic, like "Whale Watching in Southern California."

But why stop there? Why limit yourself to a magazine piece, a reprint, maybe a rewrite, and some simultaneous submissions to newspaper travel sections? There must be a dozen more angles and articles you could glean from whales, and as long as you're researching at the feasibility level anyway, why not extend that hunt and do the same basic research for many queries instead of just one?

So rather than a few hours spent finding some key facts and assuring yourself that you have a valid topic for a query, set aside a few days or a week to do the same for, say, eight queries which, by the simple multiplication of reprints, rewrites, and so on could result in 30 or 40 actual sales.

Granted, the risk is greater because the initial planning and research time is greater, and there is never an absolute certainty that any of the items will sell. But the odds are in your favor when you send out many good queries, simultaneously, about different aspects of a salable idea. A king-size payoff is also sufficiently probable to offset the uncertainties—if you start with a topic that has solid sales appeal.

You start with "whales," "gray whales," and "whale watching" at the library, to compile a list of articles that have appeared in print during the past 5 to 10 years. Do the same for books, and thumb through the recent academic papers too. At the same time, keep a list of the magazines using whale-related stories, plus the name and affiliation of every person quoted about whales, the authors of the academic papers, and the book and article writers. These form your reference/resource list for use in preparing the articles.

From this initial research you are also picking up new ideas for articles. Each of these ideas you list at the end of a spoke, which for reasons of space are limited to 8 in our example. There may be 12, 20 or 50. From gray whales in southern California you might move backward to a piece on gray whales in general, and forward to whale watching in Baja California, in the mainland United States (California and Massachusetts, mainly), and Hawaii.

While researching the general piece you may have discovered that the grays may be removed from the endangered species list. Their numbers rose from about 100 to 13,000+ since they were added to the list, so that becomes another article. How they find their way under water at night suggests a piece about echolocation, their method of orientation. And a chance encounter with the captain of the craft that caught Gigi, the only gray ever kept in captivity (at San Diego's Sea World), might lead to the eighth idea.

As the number of spokes grows, so does your reference/resource list. With each new topic, new names and articles mean new sources of information for each of the other articles, plus the possibility of tying two or several articles together, like "Whale Watching

Figure 14 Topic-Spoking: Whales

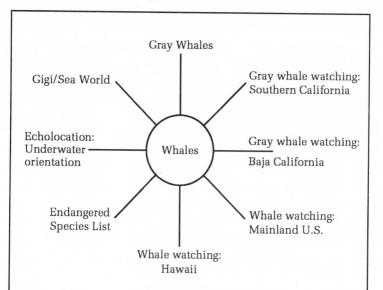

Rather than prepare an article about each topic, "topic-spoke."
Complete a feasibility study for many potential articles that share
a common research base, thus requiring progressively less basic
research for each article while expanding the amount of
information and human resources available for all of the articles.
In the above example the core information, in the center circle, is
shared by all; it concerns the whales. Moving from the core, the
writer must provide the specifics for each topic, though in
preparing the specifics for one topic, specifics about others may
become available from the same source. If an article is to be
written for each of the eight subtopics noted, all eight queries
could be sent simultaneously, since each go-ahead would result
in a different article. Usually, many articles can be written for
each subtopic, and subtopics can often be combined with each
other to produce even more articles. Multiply that potential by
the number of reprints and rewrites that could be generated from
each printed article and you can see how topic-spoking could
generate much more income from far less time expenditure than
the conventional one-idea, one-sale approach.

in the Californias," "Watching Gray Whales World-wide," or "The World's Longest Migration—Under-water."

The purpose of the extended research is (1) to see how much has been printed recently about the topic, (2) to create new spokes from the ideas emanating from the basic topic to develop into articles, (3) to compile the reference/resource list, and (4) to find a usable assortment of facts, quotes, and anecdotes for the query letters.

Once you have chosen the spokes you must determine how you will market them. A general piece on gray whales might sell to a nature or conservation magazine or even to the general-interest field if the material is extremely interesting and nonacademic. So you will complete the steps necessary to create a market list or lists, and query the top publication(s).

"Whale Watching in Baja California" might be of interest to magazines with a West Coast orientation, which you would query; to regional magazines along the coast (for a different article), which could be sent simultaneously if there is no overlap; to in-flights serving or originating from the coast, again sent simultaneously without overlap, and to newspaper travel sections across the United States.

Continue that process for each spoke. Under each, list the ways that idea could be sold: queried articles, simultaneous submissions, humor, fillers, etc.

For the queried sales, develop market lists. Likewise, for the simultaneous submissions, list the publications to be offered the manuscript once it is written. With all the potential markets listed, you can determine which idea would be offered to which publication first, thus creating an overall plan that will give you the wisest market penetration, without overlap or self-competition.

Once you have a sales plan, draw from the pool of information gathered during the extended feasibility research and prepare query letters, adding specific research to each as needed. Mail the queries. (You should also complete the research needed for the simultaneous submissions, write, and mail them.)

Can you query more than one editor at a time even though all the queries refer to gray whales? Of course, as long as you are querying about completely different articles. That's the beauty of topic-spoking. You lay out your entire marketing program for many ideas at the same time, and rather than flood just one market with many queries and submissions, you mold the topic to suit as many different markets as possible. That's how you parlay a $300 one-idea, one-sale topic into $3,000 in far less time than it would take to make ten one-shot sales.

Remember something else: As far as reprints and rewrites are concerned, there is no difference whether you sell the ideas one at a time or through topic-spoking. So that form of follow-up income yields multiple sales here too, though with so many more sales in topic-spoking, the follow-up, and subsequent sales, should also be much greater.

There's no magic to topic-spoking any more than there's magic to selling articles singly. Try it, you'll like it. As we said, it may be the best of all paths to fiscal comfort in the freelance writing world.

QUESTIONS, ANSWERS, AND ADDITIONAL THOUGHTS

Q: What kinds of ideas don't lend themselves to topic-spoking?

A: Singular, one-theme, tightly focused subjects that, once described, defy further elaboration in print.

I once wrote about an extraordinary cultural ana-
chronism in Ecuador called *pelota de guante*, a modern-day jai alai sort of game that originated in Spain
from volleyball. A huge leather glove that looked to
be twice the size of a knuckleball catcher's mitt,
bound tightly to the hand and bearing giant spike
heads on the front, was used to hit a three-pound
solid rubber ball on an irregular 60-foot court.

As colorful as it was to watch against a backdrop of
snow-capped volcanoes at 9,500 feet, the topic was
good for one or two articles in sports magazines, plus
a short in an in-flight serving Ecuador. Where did one
go from there? "The Minor Leagues of *Pelota de
Guante*"? "The Babe Ruth of the Giant Glove"? Simply too narrow for topic-spoking.

Q: How do you turn a $50 idea into $500 or $5,000?

A: By moving a local idea into the national arena.

You hear that a retired minister just graduated from
a community college, having returned to school to become a licensed vocational nurse. You interview him
to gather facts, quotes, and anecdotes. The result: $50
in Redondo Beach, where the example is a reality—if
you can find a local weekly or regional magazine
hunting for a filler.

You and America lose! You, because you turn a
megabuck idea into a minibuck sale. America, because its millions of retirees don't read of a way to
share their skills and vitality with others. You missed
some super selling markets, too—retirement, jobs,
health care—because you barely scratched the surface.

How can you turn this into big money? By looking
at the idea instead of the example, then finding six or
ten other examples related to that idea. By selling the
major article nationwide, after topic-spoking it to find

all the ways other ideas radiating from the concept could also be marketed. Then marketing them too.

How do you gather more information to see whether the idea has substance worth developing? Ask yourself what it is that others want to read about. Is it seniors returning to the health care field, in anything from nursing to gerontology?

Check to see what else is in print about your idea. Talk with knowledgeable people who deal with seniors or medically related fields to see how widespread the movement is. (It needn't be massive. The numbers might show a trend that you identified in its earliest stages.) Research by phone. Spend a few hours and dollars. Work with a reference librarian to pinpoint the key names and institutions where long-distance calls will bring quick, impressive results.

And don't reject an idea if you discover that much has been written about it already. That's good news, not bad. People, and editors, care about the topic or issue. Just find out what more needs to be said, said better, brought up to date, or clarified.

Remember, there are very few ideas that won't find a home on some printed page. And if the idea relates to people's needs or their curiosity, it will put somebody profitably in print.

———■———

*In America only the successful writer is
important, in France all writers are important,
in England no writer is important, and in
Australia you have to explain what a writer is.*
                                    Geoffrey Cotterell, 1961

CHAPTER 12

Writing
and Taxes

I f you are writing to earn income, you can also earn
by saving at tax time. To do so you must faithfully
report your earnings, deduct your business expenses,
keep receipts and records, and—if challenged, usually by audit—be able to prove that yours are business
activities rather than a hobby.

What follows is general advice culled from personal experience, talks with IRS employees while
preparing a similar segment about taxes for my writing seminar, interviews with professional tax prepar-
ers, and other books discussing the same topic. Still,
because federal (and state) tax regulations change
from time to time and this book doesn't, and your particular situation may differ from the general conditions discussed, you should seek specific advice from
the IRS or a tax consultant. (You have just read a disclaimer!)

Since most people will read this chapter seeking
information about deductions, and we have no way of
knowing about the many state and local tax demands,
the focus here will be on federal income tax, deductions, and a state of mind, plus recordkeeping.

The state of mind first. It asks the purpose of your writing.

If your purpose is to tinker with words, or write a poem now and then, or dabble, all for the fun of it and with no serious intent to sell what you create, you have a hobby. A fun but exacting hobby for which you pay all the expenses and lose virtually all the tax deductions.

PROOF OF PURPOSE

But if your purpose is to earn income, to sell what you write, even though you have fun in the doing, your expenses are deductible. Which raises two key questions: How do you prove that purpose and how do you show the expenses?

Proof of your purpose becomes necessary only if you are asked, probably at an audit, which in itself is unlikely unless your tax return looks blatantly un-businesslike, you are excessively greedy, you are dishonest, or you doggedly report losses long after you should be showing gains.

But if proof of purpose is called for, there are two important items that will show income-earning intent. One is volume of output. The second is letters of intent.

The first you prove by maintaining a mailing record of every letter and manuscript sent to potential buyers. A simple way to maintain such a record is to divide a piece of manuscript paper into three columns: *date, item sent,* and *recipient,* with sufficient room between entries to summarize the reply and any follow-up action. If all such submissions are kept in chronological order, and the pages are held together with a folder, brads, or a clip, the volume of transactions will be readily available to show upon request.

In addition, retain copies of every manuscript or letter mailed that year, plus all responses (including mass-produced rejection forms on which you should note what was rejected and when it was sent). Don't paste rejections on your wall unless you want to take your wall to the audit!

Needless to say, there must be some evidence of seriousness of purpose in the volume of items offered for sale. If you send out one query letter every few months, plus an article a year, the volume will scarcely distinguish your income-earning from a hobby. And if you try to deduct several thousand dollars of expenses against such an underwhelming marketing volume, your deductions may well be denied.

Letters of intent are more a term than an actual thing. That is, except in the rarest of occasions, there is no such thing as a letter clearly identified or labeled as a "letter of intent." Rather, these are positive replies to query letters. Often they are a note scribbled on the query itself saying "Let's see it" or "Send on spec."

What the editor is saying in giving you a positive response to a query is "I seriously intend to consider purchasing the copy you will prepare for me for publication." Thus, based on that intent, you can deduct all reasonable expenses incurred in its preparation.

Why? Because the editor cannot make a purchasing decision without reading the final copy, and you must pay certain expenses to gather information, write, and submit that final manuscript. It isn't essential that the editor buy the article for you to deduct reasonable costs. It is important only that you have queried in professional business fashion, received a positive response, and sent a final manuscript for full consideration.

A critical word in this deduction is "reasonable," for which there are as many definitions as "letters of intent." A $5,000 trip to Borneo to write a $50 article transcends reasonableness, at least where deductions are concerned. But $500 in costs for a $500 article may not be if the material gathered can be used for rewrites and reprints to earn three or four times the initial costs. Let common sense and the IRS be your guides.

KEEPING TRACK

How do you report your earnings and expenses? On Schedule C (Profit or Loss from Business or Profession) of your Form 1040 (U.S. Individual Income Tax Return), submitted at regular filing time. It is self-explanatory, in a confusing way. You may also need Form 4562 (Depreciation and Amortization) and Schedule SE (Computation of Social Security Self-Employment Tax).

Just keep a sensible account of your writing-related income and expenses as they occur, tally them up at the year's end, and adjust your 1040 by inserting the figures appropriately.

It's imperative that you keep receipts for money spent. There are a few exceptions. Tips, coin phones, and small-change items should be noted on your expense sheet when they occur but needn't be verified by receipt. Food costs can be averaged on trips if they are reasonable: so much for breakfast, lunch, and dinner. And car costs are best deducted on a per-mile basis (the IRS will give you the current figure) as long as they are logged regularly. A notebook stored in the glove compartment is perfect: Write the date, the miles traveled (or start-stop odometer readings), and how they pertain to writing.

Some other items are clearly deductible, if receipted and used to earn income by writing. Like the necessary tools: paper, envelopes, pencils, and pens. Buy stamps at the post office so you can get a receipt. Depreciate your typewriter or word processor. Deduct the ribbons, correction liquid, repair, and other supplies and direct costs.

If you use your telephone for writing-related purposes, deduct those calls but not the base rate. Cameras and tape recorders are depreciable; film, tape, needed supplies, and inexpensive accessories are normally deductible. Even a room in your house can provide numerous deductions if it is used exclusively as an office. You can request a booklet about this subject distributed free by the IRS. Use its method of calculating these deductions.

Travel costs, if necessary to research and prepare copy, are deductible—if reasonable and required. That includes getting to and fro, food, lodging, tips, laundry, and all other expenses needed to live and perform your task away from home. Entertainment too, if directly related to writing income, can be deducted.

It is far easier to justify the necessity of the travel if you have one or many letters of intent before you leave. Even query letters awaiting replies help since they show that the purpose of the trip mentioned is to write articles for publication.

What happens if you don't have letters of intent but simply take the trip and write when you return? You are usually limited to deducting proven and necessary expenses equal to the amount of money you earn. Or if you spend only a quarter of your time writing? You can deduct a maximum of 25% of your costs. Or you spend a year elsewhere to learn a new culture so you can then write a novel with that setting? Keep receipts and take the deductions when the book is in print and you are earning as much as you are claiming.

But if you're just going to the library for the day, you can't even deduct your lunch! You must spend the night away to deduct meals, unless you are paying for another's meal as an entertainment expense. If you have to pay to park, use a copier, or have a printout produced, though, those are deductible.

When can you start taking deductions? From the moment you incur expenses related to your writing income, even if the expenses precede that income. The IRS knows that a certain amount of "tooling up" is necessary for almost any business. You need a typewriter or word processor to submit query letters and manuscripts in readable fashion, for example. So it's perfectly conceivable to have many deductions without any income, and to have expenses exceed income for some months or even years while you perfect your marketing and writing skills.

But that can't continue forever. A profit (more income than expenses) at least three of the first five years is the rough guideline. Nor can the expenses be vastly out of proportion to the potential earnings without drawing a stern challenge. So you must diligently seek a profit position in your writing activities, and conduct your activities in a fashion conducive to earning a profit. Which is why a sensible, proven, businesslike process is outlined in this book that, if followed, should clearly distinguish your purpose and method as income-oriented rather than being a hobby.

You will have many more questions concerning

taxes. Horse sense and a close reading of materials easily obtainable from the Internal Revenue Service will answer 90% of them. Beyond that you may need a tax adviser or a professional preparer. Just remember that it is your duty, not just your opportunity, to claim every deduction that is rightly yours. But not a cent more.

QUESTIONS, ANSWERS, AND ADDITIONAL THOUGHTS

Q: Can you deduct the time spent writing?

A: In a word, no. Nor the time spent thinking, traveling, or laughing at the funny words you will use in humor pieces. Nor can you pay yourself a wage if you report your income as a single proprietor, which is how you will do it. So you had better use that time productively!

Q: Is this book deductible?

A: You bet. So are all the other books about freelancing—if you are buying them for the purpose of increasing your income from freelance writing. Feel free to take this note with you to your next audit. Beware if the auditor guffaws wildly after reading it. You got a guffawing auditor, nothing worse. Ask for another.

Using Schedule C

"If you are the sole owner of an unincorporated business, you must report business income and expenses on Schedule C (Form 1040)." So it begins. If you are making money or paying expenses, or both, this is how you stay honest with the Uncle. Even if you have a regular job, or many jobs, you fill in one "C" for your writing. In addition, you must keep records and receipts for expenditures, plus copies of all correspondence (particularly queries and replies) and all submitted manuscripts.

Much of the form will not pertain to you if selling your writing is the limit of your activities. Schedule C-1, "Cost of Goods Sold and/or Operations," has no bearing, nor will much of the material on the back be applicable.

From what the IRS tells me (and what I did for many years), you don't need an "employer identification number," line C, until you have employees (other than yourself!), and can use your Social Security number, the line above, for identification. Nor must you have a "business name," line B, other than your own. (In fact, if you do you will want to complete the Fictitious Business Statement at your county records office.) Your address will likely be your home, unless you have a separate office. And most use "cash" as the accounting method in E, and "cost" in F.

Part I, Income, is easy enough: List by source, then tally up the money received during that year from your writing. Include a copy of that list with your return and keep a copy for your own records. Remember, that's actual money received. Not promised, hoped for, or talked about. In the hand, through it, or in the bank.

Part II, Deduction, is more fun at tax time. Alas, the Great Collector in Washington, D.C., has no appreciation of creative talents, particularly in this area. He wants to see receipts, records, numbers, proof. So you should have been keeping these items together, to now lump by category so you can receive benefit for having paid your business expenses.

The categories where you are most likely to have expenses as a writer are bank service charges (if you keep your writing funds separate), car and truck expenses, depreciation (of equipment: typewriter, cameras, word processor, printer, etc.), dues and publications, office supplies and postage, repairs, travel and entertainment, utilities and phone, and incidental costs under other expenses. As your writing income increases, the number of categories will also increase.

Tally your income and your expenses. Subtract the smaller from the larger. If you made more than you spent, you have a profit. If not, you have a loss. Whichever, that is then posted on your regular 1040, from which the personal tax you owe is calculated.

Some IRS Suggestions That Apply to Writers

(Each item below comes directly from an IRS tax guide.)

1. Deposit all business receipts in a separate bank account and make all disbursements from that account by check. Avoid making out checks to cash. Rather, establish a petty cash fund for small expenditures.

2. Support all entries in that account with documentation. File all canceled checks, paid bills, duplicate deposit slips, and other items that support entries in your books in an orderly manner and keep them in a safe place.

3. You must keep your business books and records available at all times for IRS inspection. They must be kept until the statute of limitations for that return runs out—usually three years after the return is due or filed, or two

years from the date the tax was paid, whichever occurs later.

4. You may use a standard mileage rate instead of actual operating and fixed expenses and depreciation for using your vehicle for business. Check the current rates with the IRS.

5. Parking fees and tolls paid during business use are also deductible.

6. Travel expenses are the ordinary and necessary expenses of foreign or domestic travel away from home for your business. Under that category deductible travel expenses include air, rail, and bus fares; car expenses; fares or other costs of local transportation; baggage charges and transportation; meals and lodging when you are away from home on business; cleaning and laundry; telephone and telegraph; public stenographer's fees; tips; and other, similar business-related expenses.

7. Entertainment expenses are usually deductible if they meet three criteria: (a) You had more than a general expectation of getting income or some other specific business benefit at some future time, and (b) you did engage in business with the person being entertained during the entertainment period, and (3) the main purpose of the combined business and entertainment was the business transaction.

———■———

The writer is the Faust of modern society, the only surviving individualist in a mass age. To his orthodox contemporaries he seems a semi-madman.

Boris Pasternak, 1959

CHAPTER 13

An Example: River City, U.S.A.

In this chapter we will follow the development of an idea from its inception to sale, tracing the concepts presented in this book and, when needed, returning to review some of the exhibits used in the text that were drawn from this example.

The story concerns "River City," the setting for *The Music Man*, Meredith Willson's stage and film musical. River City is in fact Mason City, Iowa.

I chose this example even though it has now been 15 years since publication, because it is interesting to the widest number of readers and because it most closely follows our process at the developmental stages. But the example is just that: an example, not a model you must slavishly follow or that could not be improved on. There are no absolutes in freelancing, rather things that work well and consistently and others that don't work often or even at all.

AN IDEA IS BORN

The idea first emerged as a throwaway comment in a conversation, in this case over cards.

"But they didn't write a mus-i-CAL about your home town," went the banter from a long-suffering resident of the Cement Capital of Northern Iowa, or so we dubbed Mason City. None of us knew a whit more about the town than that our friend came from it and so did cement. Since he was a football player, he suffered from the association.

"A musical?" I asked, with wit and cunning. I was from Chicago, setting and focus of many a musical, which I chose to ignore. "What musical did they write about Mason City?"

"*The Music Man*," he said, quietly taking the hand and winning the pot. "That was River City, U.S.A."

Further probing hit stone. Yes, he was sure about Mason City being the setting. No, he didn't know Meredith Willson. No, he really didn't know much more about it than that. He smiled and dealt another hand.

Sharp writers pounce on such tidbits, pluck out the selling features, wing off to the library, peck out the prose, and pocket the results.

I almost forgot about it.

In truth, had I not by chance seen and stopped at the Iowa Tourism Bureau in downtown Chicago a few weeks later, this chapter would be about Idaho or Ecuador.

The matronly employee behind the counter looked stymied when I asked her "Was Mason City really the setting for *The Music Man*?"

"Heavens, boy, I'm sure I wouldn't know," she replied, smiling and looking for a primer to see whether Mason City was even in Iowa. Clearly she had never been west of Pulaski Avenue. "But it should say in here," she said, handing me some brochures and a map of north-central Iowa.

I found one reference: Mason City was the location for the writing of Meredith Willson's *The Music Man*, or something as prosaically turgid. It was going to take work to ferret a windfall out of Mason City. My response was typical: I wrote about something else.

Still, as spring approached the thought of driving to Iowa for a weekend looked ever more appealing. So I decided to dig in, do it right, take a fun trip, make it pay, and turn the results over in print as painlessly and profitably as possible.

The first thing I did was ask what I really wanted to know. Was there anything in Mason City mentioned in *The Music Man* or sufficiently reminiscent of River City to lure a traveler that way? Or had the site so changed that the story would be "River City Gone Modern!"? If Meredith Willson had grown up there, how much of that past could still be identified? Was there anything nearby to add luster to the location? The minimum I'd need to justify the trip and writing time would be some physical or nostalgic link between the city and the musical. So that's what I'd seek first.

YOU GOTTA KNOW THE TERRITORY

Unfortunately, I had to be the only living American who had never seen the play or movie! At best I could mumble a few of the lyrics. (I was living in South America when the movie made its debut. When I got back it wasn't around—nor were VCRs.)

So a hunt for the script was next. Have you ever tried to find a script in a library? Yet the librarian had heard that a nearby college was staging the play, and a kind call gave me a name to contact. It was less easy to persuade an-academic to let me borrow a script overnight; I pledged to build a new wing or something if it was wrinkled and not returned by dawn! I rush-read and copied every reference to River City, the people, and the time, plus lyrics and other key phrases I thought would fit into an article.

After reading the script I felt that if there was anything at all worth seeing in Mason City, there were enough references and good writing in the script to build an article around. Thus I began the usual pre-writing process built on the confidence that the subject would result in sales.

My working question that the article would answer: "What will today's visitor to Mason City find that will remind him of River City in *The Music Man*?" If I wanted to get paid for the answer, I had to find the kinds of readers who would benefit from or at least be interested in knowing that answer.

The Market List

So I made two lists: (1) those benefited and (2) those particularly interested. (If an article meets a need—how to get rich, become beautiful, write a will, woo a mate—it will have higher commercial value than one that simply incites interest. I assume that if someone benefits, he will be interested, but not necessarily the reverse.)

My lists read as follows:

Those Benefited

Iowa tourism groups
Mason City

businesses in Mason City and nearby
conveyances bringing folks to Mason City:
  cars and RVs
  buses
  trains
  airlines
travelers living nearby
those planning to travel in or through Iowa

Those Particularly Interested

armchair/general travelers
Music Man fans
followers of Meredith Willson
nostalgia buffs
older folks
historians
musicians
actors/those in musicals
people in general
Midwesterners

The first list is the hottest selling prospects. They have a vested interest in the subject and will read with more than passing attention if my article appears; therefore the editors of the publications they buy will be particularly interested in acquiring it.

In an ideal situation I would take a subject, approach it from as many different angles as I could find, write a query offering a distinct manuscript from each angle, and live happily ever after. In the real world, particularly with a topic as narrow as Mason City/River City, I had to carefully select approaches and markets. Thus I made a notation by each kind of reader to seek the best markets for my articles. These are the concerns I had about each category:

- *Iowa tourism groups*: the state bureau, local Chambers of Commerce, and the tour agencies. Not promising. Probably don't buy from outsiders (though worth a letter to check; rates?). Travel agencies in Iowa probably more interested in sending their locals to Chicago, NY, etc. Move down on list. For rainy day.

- *Mason City*: Check when you go, or before, to see whether booklet, local tour or history guide, exists. If not, good idea. Probably have to self-publish; how would you handle local distribution? Marketing problem. See whether articles can be converted, whole thing sold to local hustler.

- *Businesses in Mason City and nearby*: Same as Mason City. Won't buy articles but would be sales outlets for local booklet.

- *Conveyances bringing folks to Mason City*:

  cars and RVs: yep, good topic that would provide a place to drive to and visit. Include other sites in 50-mile radius since they'd need a car to see them. Look into state AAA publication, national car magazines.

  buses: Are there magazines to read in buses, such as in-flights? Or magazines put out by Greyhound? How many will take a bus just to see Mason City?

  trains: same as buses.

  airlines: only Ozark. Have an in-flight magazine? If so, good market.

- *Travelers living nearby*: good sources, regional

travel magazines of Iowa or the Midwest in general. Much more likely that locals will head that way or detour.

- *Those planning to travel in or through Mason City*: impossible to isolate. Will read the piece because of *The Music Man*, might actually travel to site if already heading in that direction. Good market.

- *Armchair and general travelers*: same as previous listing. Must feature visuals for armchair group who will never see it in person, less on motel rates and road instructions. Add specialty travel, with other primary orientations: sailing, hunting, fishing, etc. If other travel-linked topics deserve an article, tie in the River City angle: "Lazy Day's Fishin' in River City, U.S.A."

- *"Music Man" fans*: the best target but hard to isolate. Includes almost anybody who saw the movie or stage production. Some would read entertainment/theater-related publications.

- *Followers of Meredith Willson*: same as "Music Man" fans, probably, plus those interested in radio broadcast/history. See if "old-time radio" has magazines buying pieces.

- *Nostalgia buffs*: good market. Setting was small-town Iowa in 1912. Most read general or retirement magazines, plus specialties.

- *Older folks*: same as nostalgia. Retirement publications. To be age of characters in musical would be in 70s and up.

- *Historians*: Here the approach would be Mason City as it actually was in 1912 compared to the way *The Music Man* paints it. Perhaps seen through another 10-year-old boy (Willson was 10

in the year it was set). Doubt that history magazines would be interested; less likely they pay
enough. But a very interesting approach for a
general/retirement publication. Write first article
from contemporary setting, check out availability
of data in Mason City, consider a second article
from this slant.

- *Musicians*: both the actual music and the "band"
  theme of the story. Tie-in with band festivals in
  the town. Or music as it was taught (or not) in
  Mason City in 1912 with the way it is pictured.
  Or Willson as an example of smalltown music
  training, comparing him with other musicians of
  like training.

- *Actors/those in musicals*: very few publications
  specifically directed here.

- *People in general*: outside of general travel, perhaps the best source for sales. Almost everybody
  knows the stage show or film, relates to the past
  and small towns. If done in a light spirit, upbeat
  like the music, it would be a welcome balance
  piece for almost any publication with readers
  who know about *The Music Man*.

- *Midwesterners*: same as travelers living nearby.
  Yet regionals outside Iowa or nearby not likely to
  use it to attract their readers to another locale!

From the above lists and notes I selected five markets,
three of which were composites. The first three I
planned to pursue immediately, the last two were for
follow-ups:

general travel/cars: the most logical, widest selection of travel markets

local/Midwestern travel: fewer publications

retirement/nostalgia/general reader: good, broad
   market

historians: if data available

musicians: also, if information available, markets
   pay enough

In addition, I planned to rewrite one or several of the
articles into newspaper travel pieces to be submitted
(where no overlap existed) to editors simultaneously
across the United States and Canada.

For our purposes in this book, let's focus now on
the top magazine category—general travel/cars—and
see, later, how that article became a different piece for
newspaper distribution.

My next task was to compile a market list of magazines in the general travel/cars area so I could set up
some order for query submission. I turned to *Writer's
Market* for the information necessary for evaluation.

From a longer list I am including the six below as
they appeared some years back, since they provide
enough information for you to follow my thought process at that time:

- *Travel*, Managing Editor, Robert H. Rufa, Travel
  Bldg., Floral Park, NY 11001. Pays on acceptance, $50-$300, query, monthly, 1,000-2,500
  wds., cities preferred, color pix best.

- *Travel and Leisure*, Editor-in-Chief, Caskie Stin-
  nett, 132 W. 31st St., NYC, NY 10001. Pays on acceptance, $500-$3,000, query, bimonthly, 1,000-
  3,000 wds.; interested in Iowa?

- *Holiday*, Managing Editor, Sandi Servaas, 1100
  Waterway Blvd., Indianapolis, IN 46202. Pays on
  publication, $50-$1,000, query, monthly, 1,000-
  2,000 wds., submit 300-word summary of idea,
  qualifications, info on pix.

- *Motor News*, Travel Editor, Len Barnes, 150 Bagley Ave., Detroit, MI 48226. Pays on acceptance, $100-$175, query suggested, monthly, 800-1,200 wds.
- *RV World*, Editor, Jim Matthews, 16200 Ventura Blvd., Encino, CA 91316. Pays on publication, $50/page, query, monthly, 1,800-3,000 wds.; focus on RV interests in/near Mason City.
- *Canadian Motorist*, Editor, Jerry Tutunjian, 2 Carlton St., Toronto 2, Ont., Canada. Pays on acceptance, $40-$100, query, bimonthly, 800-2,000 wds., must send international reply coupon with SAE for reply, buys first Canadian rights.

My task was to shuffle the list into the order most likely to yield a sale at the highest earning level with the least amount of time/expense involved.

Since it is foolish to query or submit original work to a publication that pays on publication, the list was first sorted into two levels:

Pay on Acceptance

Travel

Travel and Leisure

Motor News

Canadian Motorist

Pay on Publication

Holiday

RV World

Now we must rearrange the top four by (1) what they pay and (2) other factors.

The reshuffling by pay leaves us:

Travel and Leisure ($500–$3,000)
Travel ($50–$300)
Motor News ($100–$175)
Canadian Motorist ($40–$100)

Then the frequency of publication. Here we find *Travel* and *Motor News* are monthlies; the others, bimonthlies. Our chances of a sale are twice as good to the monthlies—but the enormous pay difference keeps *Travel and Leisure* our primary target. All that remains is the rights.

Both *Travel* and *Travel and Leisure* buy first North American serial rights, *Motor News* wants first rights, and *Canadian Motorist* buys first Canadian rights. Nothing to change the order here—but I'm thinking of moving *Canadian Motorist* down to the second-level list, to offer reprints and rewrites later. (A gut feeling: they will buy seconds.)

So it's settled: Query *Travel and Leisure* first, *Travel* second, and *Motor News* third with a general/auto travel approach about visiting the modern-day River City, U.S.A.

Remember that while I'm concentrating on one approach only in this chapter, a comprehensive sales campaign would include a similar market feasibility for many approaches—local/Midwestern travel, retirement/nostalgia/general reader, historian, and musician, in this case. For each category I would select a top market for initial querying, with lesser markets for later queries or for reprint/rewrite sales. Since each approach is different—and an article resulting from each would require different copy—all the queries (to the top market on each list) could be sent simultaneously.

Library Research

Having defined my approaches and primary markets, I then researched to see where, when, and how the topic had been written about before, and what additional information I would need to prepare my own salable copy.

Equally as important, particularly where the topic had yet to appear in print or had received scant coverage, I had to see whether information was available to prepare a piece from each approach proposed.

After all, in the query I'm going to promise an article and mention possible contents of that article to show that I can deliver what I promise. The last thing I want to do is make a baseless promise and have to beg out later, or just not come through at all.

So the first thing I looked for was other articles or books about Mason City/River City, under those headings or under *The Music Man*, Meredith Willson, Iowa, musicals, and movie reviews.

The card catalog at a large university is where I began, though for recent commercial magazines I suspected I'd have to go to the city or county library, since they are usually better stocked with popular serials.

I searched the subject and author listings for books, cross-references, and microfilm or microfiche notations. Then I went to the stacks to the numbers listed to see what else was lingering in that literary neighborhood that might shed related light on my topic.

Next I headed for the *Reader's Guide to Periodical Literature*, checking first the magazines listed against my list of primary markets, plus all other magazines I was considering from the first (pay on acceptance) level. Again, I checked the various Mason City/River City headings, noting the articles during the past five years.

I found two.

"Is Main Street Still There?" asked the *Saturday Review* on Jan. 17, 1970, in a five-page, personalized impression of contemporary Mason City. Almost nothing to meet my needs.

"Concerned Community Citizens Move to Ban Blue Movies," in *Life* (Aug. 28, 1970), was more generous factually about the Mason City/River City connection, though its main focus was far afield.

It was obvious that my idea hadn't been overused recently. That gave me a legitimate concern: surely I wasn't the first to think of the connection, but was the fact that nothing was in print proof there was nothing to say? That the musical was about some mythical town totally unlike Mason City? More research. . .

Surely Mason City would have been in the spotlight when the musical opened on Broadway, and back in the news when the movie came out. I checked the opening dates of each to see what the reviews said about Mason City. Then I returned to the *Reader's Guide* for articles between the musical's debut and 1969.

Following Brooks Atkinson's opening night review (Dec. 19, 1957) in the *New York Times*, 12 reviews appeared in the *Reader's Guide* from 1957–59, plus an interview with Willson. Ten magazine reviews also followed the movie's release in 1961. Another review of the musical, in *Dance* (August 1965), and an article, "At Home with Meredith Willson," in *American Home*, September 1960, were the remainder of the articles in listed publications from 1957–74.

The purpose of my periodical research was to identify other articles in magazines that overlapped on my subject, to avoid querying those that had carried articles about a return to Mason City to find River City. (None had.) It was also my purpose to be able to pluck from others' research sufficient information to write a knowledgeable query, to know that I could produce an article from my premise, and to build up facts and names to check in Mason City, if the trip materialized.

Sadly, I learned virtually nothing about present-day Mason City from all the material in print combined, other than that it was where Willson grew up, there was no Harold Hill, the river is a creek dried up much of the year, and that the pool hall, the Pleazol, did exist. Not much for a full article.

Meredith Willson was the pivotal element in the story. It made sense to call him. Yet to be fully prepared for a solid interview I needed to know more about him. Back to the library and the biographical source books!

The *Biography Index* is a gold mine, so I started with the current edition and worked backward to see when Willson was mentioned. Bingo! Eighteen listings: twice in *Current Biography*, three books he had written (one called *But He Doesn't Know the Territory*), and so on. A real time-saving godsend.

I checked *Current Biography* before calling Willson, and prepared a five-question interview.

Since I was then living in Cook County, Illinois, I called the *Chicago Tribune*'s information desk for his address and phone number, which they supplied. I called him the following day, to no avail. He was in

Europe on a conducting/rest tour and could not be reached for several months!

All that remained was to verify the current status of the information I had. Four sources came to mind in Mason City: the Chamber of Commerce, the newspaper, the library, and the historical society. My research funds being, as always, depleted, I decided to try them by telephone in that order, hoping the C of C would firm up the facts and I'd visit the others in person, if necessary.

The Chamber came through! I needed to know precisely what visitors to Mason City could see that was mentioned in *The Music Man* as well as the places that were still intact from Willson's youth. The contact confirmed four key items: Marion the Librarian was Willson's mother, the old library still stood, though it was now the Iowa Kempfer Mutual Insurance building, the Willson home was little changed down the street from Willow Creek (the "river" of River City), and the Pleazol, the source of so much trouble—the pool hall—not only had existed, but there was a marble nameplate in the sidewalk where it had stood. (Now they played pool four doors away.)

Still, I had only one person's word about the facts around which my query would be built. Better to get confirmation before than to try to explain why I didn't later. I called the local newspaper, told them of the article I was writing about Mason City, and asked if they would mind confirming or expanding on some facts I had gathered in my research. Five minutes, full confirmations, and a few additional items paid well for that phone call.

I had more than enough to write the query letter, plus numerous contacts once I reached Mason City— if or when I received a positive reply.

THE QUERYING PROCESS

Now all that separated me from fame, fortune, and a trip to the cement haven was an affirmative reply to a letter I'd yet to write.

Travel and Leisure was the first magazine on my list. I had two reservations about it. One, it was a bimonthly, which meant it used half as much copy as other travel magazines. And from what I saw on its pages, Iowa seemed a long way from the core of its interest. But a shot at $3,000 beckoned, and even the $500, on the soft side, was better than anybody else paid.

So I trotted over to the library (actually, I rode a bike), read the key articles in its last three issues, stacked the facts I knew about Mason City/River City in the most alluring fashion, and queried. (The copy of that letter is lost but must have been nearly the same as the query to *Travel* in Figure 6. Once I've written and edited a query, if it continues to read well and is the best selling tool I can produce, I alter it only enough to meet the new editor's needs.)

The query was rejected. Their loss. Who wouldn't want to know more about this topic, as filtered through my all-seeing eyes and magic prose? Apparently *Travel and Leisure* readers!

Travel magazine was next. Let's look at the write-up in *Writer's Market '74* to see why I wrote the query letter as I did:

TRAVEL, Travel Bldg., Floral Park NY 11001. Managing Editor: Robert H. Rufa. For "active travelers." Monthly. Circulation: approximately 600,000. Buys first North American serial rights. Pays on acceptance. Will send a sample copy to a writer on request. "Study magazine. Remember that we work 4 months in advance." Query first. Enclose S.A.S.E.

Nonfiction: Wants what-to-do-and-see material in a particular locale or city, but not single sites, with costs and prices worked in wherever appropriate. Information on dining and accommodations is most helpful. Travel may take place either in U.S. or foreign country. Articles should deal with areas or cities rather than museums, landmarks, etc. Length: 1,000 to 2,500 words. Buys photos with articles, preferably with people in the scenes. B&w glossy. 5 x 7 or larger. 35mm original transparencies or larger. "We are forced to return otherwise acceptable editorial material if photos are of poor quality or if they are improperly captioned, etc. Though we rarely buy photos without a ms, we don't mind hearing from a photographer with an extensive slide or b&w print file, on the possibility of a photo essay or as a source for material." Pays $50 to $150 for a b&w piece, depending on length. Pays $150 to $300 for color.*

The area emphasis seemed encouraging and would allow me to include the nearby sites. On a map I drew a circle around Mason City to show all the oddities within 50 miles from which to select the most interesting attractions.

The description in *Writer's Market* also emphasized the need for many good 35mm slides to earn top dollar. So I'd mention their existence in the query and plan to spend extra photo time in Mason City to make their existence a reality.

And since *Travel* bought first rights, I'd be able to sell seconds, or reprints, after the piece was published.

A close reading of the last three issues showed that the editor enjoyed humorous articles, a light touch evenly spread. *The Music Man* itself was upbeat and

*(From 1974 *Writer's Market*, reprinted with permission of Writer's Digest Books.)

fun, so I could write that way. Even more, to show him that I could inject controlled levity, I'd do so in the query, with a fast-paced, fact-filled letter similar to the content of the better articles I had reviewed.

Following those loose guidelines I composed a query letter designed to sell my idea—and me as the writer—to Mr. Robert Rufa, the managing editor. The actual letter appears in Chapter 6 as Figure 6.

Let's review that letter now to see why it reads as it does.

It's as important to start with a lead in a query as it is in an article. The lyrics to one of the songs set the stage perfectly.

I kept the paragraphs short because *Travel* did the same. And the focus was on what the article would cover and how: facts written with humor.

The impression I wanted to give Rufa was that I had been there—or at least that I was fully informed about Mason City/River City. To expand the regional theme, I included the other attractions: rare relict mice, fossils, and Hamlin Garland's home, among others—items left woefully unexplained in other, lesser magazines.

In claiming not to toot my horn, I did—my publication total, excluding newspaper items. Finally, I included a question in the last paragraph to give the editor something to answer, then closed with a bit of humorous fluff that showed, clearly, that I was fighting to keep the mirth in tight restraint for *Travel* readers.

I spent a good deal of time writing the query, picking out the most important points to make, verifying the facts, smoothing out the prose, editing and moving words, and creating the right tone.

(Alas, not quite enough time. How I came up with 25 years since the musical had made its debut, when it should have been 17, I don't know. But neither did the editor, fortunately.)

It worked. I sent the letter in early March. Robert Rufa replied almost immediately: "Can you imagine a New York publication interested in a band town in rural Iowa? But it looks good for our June issue!"

So June it was. I'd tentatively planned the trip for a few weeks off. Time to call the Chamber of Commerce and arrange to meet a helper who would point out the Willson and *Music Man* site. I'd visit the neighboring countryside myself, camera and notebook in hand. I reread the feasibility material, formed the questions I wanted to ask, and got on to other writing until the day of departure.

ON-SITE RESEARCH

After all this preparation, the visit itself was somewhat anticlimactic. I found the few things there were to see, photographed them, and combed the countryside, wandering through park after park, splashing in the memorable Clear Lake, and filling two days with hustle and photos.

I'd hoped to interview Willson's contemporaries, but the three I met were slow on recall. Meredith was in his 70s by then, and so were his childhood friends. The ones I found were friendly but tired, and that avenue led nowhere. I was left to gather impressions and confirm facts. In truth, the highlight was the set of baseball games I was dragooned into catching the nights I visited, my glove having been spotted by a desperate but eagle-eyed shortstop who stopped me short at an intersection!

Thank God for the thorough feasibility study. I had enough material for a solid story, and the on-site verification and the backup photos gave the long-range research local credence. Most important, because of my solid preparation I did ferret out what I needed to produce selling copy. I knew by the time I arrived what had to be confirmed, the answers I had to get, and the contacts I had to make in person—like folks at the local newspaper and Chamber of Commerce— should I need follow-up assistance later. Most important, I didn't panic when the interviews fell through. I did other things, among them enjoying myself in a lovely place full of memories perfectly captured by the musical. I went to research an article and have fun. Did both.

WRITING THE ARTICLES

I returned from Mason City, waited for my aging throwing arm to recover, and wrote the article you can read in Appendix A. I'd do it better now, 15 years later, but Rufa liked it, and Meredith Willson sent a kind note lauding its charm and veracity.

As for putting words on paper, I typed out the rough block, starting somewhere around paragraph three, and kept typing, leaving spaces where facts might fit in, until I had completed three or four pages of very rough copy. I went back, moved the paragraphs around, dug out the quotes (mostly from the script) and facts, and filled in the spaces. Then I wrote a page of leads, perhaps a dozen, until I found one that captured both the reader's interest and the sense of where I was going with the piece.

It struck me about then that this article had to be upbeat, a march in tune with the spirit of the musical, so I stepped up the pace, pruned out a peck of prose, and finally had it reading as it should. I gave it a final word-by-word check—do I mean that? can it be said better? does it flow smoothly?—before setting it aside, to be reread two days later. (That sounds good, but I never wait two days. Next morning is good enough.) No reason to dally then. It's about as good as it'll get. Keep it any longer and I'll cut out the best parts. So I typed it up and sent it off by late April. About five hours total.

TOPIC-SPOKING THE MASON CITY ARTICLE

To this point I followed the standard process: idea (what exists in Mason City to remind us of River City in *The Music Man?*), query to *Travel*, go-ahead, manuscript written and sent, article in print, and rewrites for newspaper travel sections (the *Washington Post* example is Appendix B).

But suppose I had decided to topic-spoke the idea at the outset—which is exactly what I would have decided had I not still been developing the concept. Rather than sending off a sole query, I would have spent more time at the feasibility stage developing other article topics with the same or a similar root. For example, two things are certain about the Mason City/River City piece. I would have to get to know both the city and musical well and I would have to visit north-central Iowa, to gather information and take photographs on site.

So I might have drawn up a list of potentially salable article topics that could logically come from a more intimate knowledge of the script and the location, as in the following paragraph. Most of these ideas have already been mentioned; they emerged during the feasibility study. The difference is that now I am gathering information about them as well as

Mason City/River City before I do any writing, rather than returning to them, one at a time, after I have sold the *Music Man* article.

Possible Article Ideas about Mason City/River City

- *history* piece, city as it was in 1912
- *music* as it was actually taught in 1912 in Mason City, Iowa: Were there really Harold Hills? How many "Willsons" came from that period/background?
- *"River City"* today: How close is it to an "average American town"?
- *Music Man*: How much of River City exists in Mason City today? What is there for the visitor to see/feel?

North-Central Iowa

- *Clear Lake*, now and historically
- What kind of *person* emerges from "backlands Iowa": profile, statistics, famous and infamous, compared to rest of U.S.?
- "Little Brown *Church* in the Vale"—the town disappeared, the church stayed: history, function, future?
- *cement* industry and an Iowa city: economic, environmental, social impact; future?

It's far more logical and economical to pool the information at the outset than to have to revert to history six or eight times. By having basic information at hand from which all articles can draw, as symbolized by the circle around the central crossing of the spokes, developing eight solid queries may take less

Figure 15 Topic-Spoking: Mason City

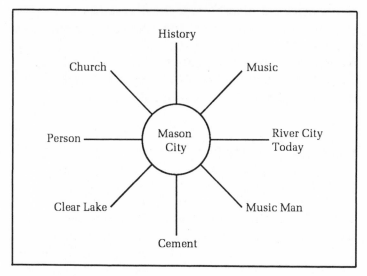

than half the time it would if each were developed separately, at different times.

Then too, my chance of receiving a go-ahead from eight different queries is far greater than from one. Say that two did respond favorably. I would complete the research and write those while I continued to query the other six. In completing the research for the two, the additional information I encountered would add more material to the pool—more facts, more names for interviews, more anecdotes—to strengthen my queries. Or more slants from which new queries could be written.

Another factor too: I would be covering a far wider writing/selling market by topic-spoking than I could have by querying one at a time. The original idea, based on *The Music Man*, would sell best to magazines with general readership. With seven other approaches being pursued simultaneously, the basic material could also be sold to magazines about history, music, sociology, sailing, religion, cement, business, and so on. Even better, not only could it be resold, rewritten, syndicated, and later made into a book, as could any other article, by topic-spoking that could be done eight ways at once!

REPRINTS AND REWRITES

If it sold once, why not sell it again and again as a reprint? That's the idea behind Figure 13 in Chapter 10. While that example is fictitious, it follows the process for reprints and rewrites outlined in the chapter. It is written precisely as I would have done it, including the offer of photos, a box or sidebar to update the article whenever it was used, and a copy of the original to facilitate typesetting—as well as my control over payment if the latter doesn't arrive.

Mind you, this letter can be sent simultaneously or when you get to it to as many likely reprint markets as you can find. There is no exclusivity to the use of the article. The article will be sent as is, with the additional items the editor selects—photo, box, original manuscript. But there is no rewriting involved. Just more income from labor expended.

An example of a rewrite of the River City story is in Appendix B. The *Travel* piece was written first, and the item sold to newspaper travel sections, including the *Washington Post*'s, was a rewrite. It began with the same material and approached it from a slightly different angle. Many of the same facts reappear; new material is added.

Because the newspaper version appeared after the *Travel* article had been in print, the difference in copy is far less than it would be if the two were in print in similar publications or at about the same time. In a sense, the newspaper travel version is, temporally, a reprint so it needn't be different at all. Yet you may want to study how they differ to see how the same basic material can be reworked to yield a new, fresh product.

MIXED MARKETS

Within the magazine field itself we identified many markets: general, travel, history, music, in-flight, etc. In addition to magazine and newspaper travel, we might also sell the material to newspaper weekly supplements, as copy for brochures or booklets, as a book, or as a sequel for a musical or a dramatic presentation. The photography might also be sold separately, as the core of photojournalism pieces, for ads or soft line greeting cards, and so on. While paying attention to the rights issues, imagination carries good ideas far.

SELLING IT ABROAD

It's hard to imagine some backlander in Bolivia or Borneo convincing a spouse to take a vacation trip to Iowa. Some topics don't cross the sea all that easily.

Yet in those lands where *The Music Man* has played, the article might be well received. The story itself transcends cultural boundaries. A contemporary look at its setting in rural America could interest overseas readers and editors. The problem would be finding where the show had played and which editors would pay for the article.

I could have checked with the script distributors, of course, to see where the show has been presented and start from there, or I could have gone directly to the syndicates to see whether they were interested in offering my article and photos to editors worldwide. The worst that could happen? The syndicates wouldn't carry it. The best? A gusher waiting to be tapped. How would I know which it was—or something in between—unless I tried? Send a query letter to one syndicate at a time until the list runs out.

PHOTOS

I sold six b/w shots to the newspaper travel sections, for about $60–$75 total, though they don't itemize the amounts paid for copy or photographs.

Travel magazine used one small b/w of the Pleazol marble name slab—the same shot, taken from about five angles, that two newspapers bought. They used a color slide of a steam locomotive from the early railroad center in East Park, as a reminder of the days circa 1912. Fortunately, I had taken photos of anything that looked interesting and old, probably including some well-tempered tourists.

But the third photo I didn't have. They wanted a big brass band as colorful as can be, marching down Main Street, "as many reds and bright colors as possible." I had gone early in a torrid spring, to beat the lead time for a June issue—well before bands graced the center street. A call went to the local Mason City newspaper. Eureka again! They had it: a tightly cadenced red-vested band led by a high school lovely smiling through her pompoms. They sent the color print, it sped express to Floral Park, and the article was presentably dressed for nationwide acclaim!

(Thank God for a few moments of handshaking at the newspaper office while I was there!)

Any points to share? Nope. I barely scrape through photographically. Go to a seminar that explains the basics of picture taking, buy a used 35mm camera, practice plenty on b/w film, take far more pictures than you need on site, know what you need before you go but open your mind to more when you're there, and get names and addresses of the key models you photo, for captions and in case you need a release later. Think visual when you write; think copy when you photo. If that doesn't drive you crazy, it should produce salable copy and salable photos.

QUESTIONS, ANSWERS, AND ADDITIONAL THOUGHTS

Parting Words

If you want to be published and you can write, you may still never be in print. And that's a shame, because the culprit is most likely ignorance about how to sell—an ignorance that is curable. One proven cure, with only lucrative side effects, is what you've been reading in this book.

There's no magic to getting into print. It's hard work, but it's doable by almost everybody. If you have something to say, say it to everyone. If you want to make money, writing and selling can satisfy that desire. If you want to leave something that is creatively yours to your grandchildren's grandchildren, do it in print.

What I've told you works. I've been telling it to others like you for years and have seen hundreds and hundreds of people publish by utilizing the techniques I've explained. Now make them work for you. Get going; get writing; get publishing. I wish you well. We need to hear what you have to say.

———■———

The maker of a sentence launches out into the infinite and builds a road into Chaos and old Night, and is followed by those who hear him with something of wild, creative delight.

Emerson, 1834

Appendix A

LAND OF THE MUSIC MAN

by Gordon Lee Burgett

(as submitted to *Travel* magazine for use
in June 1974)

River City, U.S.A., is alive and hiding in north-central Iowa, much as Harold Hill described it to the nation in Meredith Willson's 1957 smash hit, *The Music Man.*

"Ya got trouble, friend,
Right here, I say,
Trouble right here in River City!"

The trouble, you recall, was a billiards hall called the Pleazol, and the cure was a marching band—instruments bought, sight unseen, from one Harold Hill.

If you too laughed and applauded the author's foot-tapping imagination, then wend your way to Mason City, Iowa, walk north on the west side of Federal Avenue from Central Park, and look down. There tiled in the pavement for all to see: PLEAZOL! (Trouble lurks a few doors away, where billiards continue to "threaten" the morals of the local youth.)

Mason City is bigger now and laced with multi-storied evidences of modernity, but River City still lingers all around. With a bit of imagination you can almost hear young Meredith playing his flute before the Kiwanis Club at the Cerro Gordo Hotel as he did one Wednesday afternoon that year of 1912, and see a well of memories filling up, to flood America through 76 trombones 45 years later, with enough warm-hearted, fast-talking corn to play every night since somewhere in the world.

"The land of *The Music Man*" is more than a city full of musical nostalgia; it's dozens of wooded, watered campgrounds, Iowa's third-largest lake and key resort only eight miles to the west, and enough flat-land variety to delight any visitor, particularly one convinced beforehand that "there's nothing out there but corn and more corn."

Still, newcomers will want to find those trade-marks that led to the musical's particular Midwest flavor, like the footbridge, Marion the Librarian, and Willson's home. A task to test the seasoned scout, mind you, for although Mason City proudly acknowl-edges the distinction and scatters occasional signs in recognition, it leaves the infrequent curious to their own designs.

Marion was Mrs. Willson, at least in spirit, and her old haunt, the library, now houses an insurance firm. The Willson home sits five houses north of Willow Creek, east side of Pennsylvania Avenue—it's painted green. And the footbridge . . . well, that's a longer story.

A few blocks east of the Willson home, past the first-rate art museum and new library, is the "Music Man Bridge," looking every bit like the span which appeared in the movie that premiered in Mason City in 1962. Alas, it's not the original. The bridge Willson knew sat in East Park a few blocks farther east. It caved in 24 years back, and a replacement now stands on the original site. Since it's far less impressive, tourists are pointed to the "Music Man Bridge" and left to make the wrong assumption.

Hunt as you will—cemetery, diaries, the memories of old-timers—Harold Hill is not to be found. In fact, he never really existed, or as Willson says, "He's so many people I remember different ones every time I see the show." But his spirit returns every June, usually the second Tuesday—after school is out and right before haying—when the North Iowa Band Festival fills the streets, parks, and shopping centers with a hundred marching bands, Miss North Iowa queen hopefuls, standard-bearers, pom-pom lasses, and drum majors and majorettes. Outsiders fill the motels and crowds line the streets to cheer the school-year-ending finale.

Four times Meredith Willson has been recalled to lead the June highlight. In 1953, then known for playing the piccolo with Sousa and the flute with Toscanini, he helped celebrate the city's centennial. In 1958, he was cheered for the success of the musical, and it was more of the same five years back. But in 1962 a special thrill accompanied his visit: the first showing of the movie The Music Man, with a real live Harold Hill in tow, Robert Preston.

Willson may return again this June, but if all goes as planned, he definitely will mount the podium in 1976 to lead those 76 symbolic trombones in a spine-tingling salute to our nation's 200th anniversary.

Other special events in north-central Iowa include the River City Barbershop Annual Parade of Quartets in March and the Northern Iowa Fair in August, in

Mason City, and the gala Fourth of July celebration, Iowa's largest, in nearby Clear Lake.

In fact, many if not most Mason City visitors camp in one of the two popular state parks at Clear Lake; the larger site on the southern shore called Clear Lake State Park, or the more wooded, peninsular McIntosh Woods on the opposite side, near Ventura.

Not only does the lake live up to its name (thanks to a sewer line that rims the water), it has yielded the state's largest muskie, and sizable catches of northern pike, walleye, bass, perch, and catfish. Swimming and boating are the most common summer activities, while the winter lures almost as many visitors, to ice fish and para-sail.

Pilot Knob State Park, 30 miles northwest near Forest City, draws a different crowd, since its half-hidden Dead Man's Lake is too acidic to support fish. Its lofty glacial draft rises 1,500 feet, the second-highest peak in Iowa, affording the curious a view of 35 miles. Hiking and camping are its main attractions, although the scientific spend hours or days hunting for two oddities found almost exclusively in or near the park's floating sphagnum bog: a relict mouse called the red-backed vole and a carnivorous plant that feeds like the Venus's-flytrap, the sundew.

Beed's Lake, to the south near Hampton, sits at the edge of an airport where the air-campers land and hike a few blocks to the side of a quiet lake. The water is completely surrounded by the state preserve, and a popular sand beach faces the land dike, with two footbridges that cut the water diagonally, markedly increasing the fishing shoreline. This summer the stock should be legal size; the lake was drained two years back to kill off the carp and suckers. Once before, during World War II, the plug by the 40-foot horizontally layered, varicolored stone dam was lifted to free the water, so the rich bottom land could be farmed. The park and campground sit comfortably away from noise and traffic, five country miles from U.S. 65 linking Mason City to Des Moines.

Just as attractive are the many small, unhurried, yet clean and well-appointed campsites and parks found in most small towns or, like Pioneer Park near Brownville, in areas so remote you almost turn back three times before stumbling on the backwoods holding that once was the motorboat haven of the county—until its dam broke and the lake reverted to fertile cropland. What remains are bass so large that knowing anglers seldom leave untended the Cedar River shores.

During the Civil War a wooden Congregational church in the now defunct town of Bradford (near Nashua) heard a song first sung to its flock by the composer and his singing class. It was called "The Little Brown Church in the Vale," and to this well-preserved chapel thousands journey these days to be married or baptized. The boyhood home of the writer Hamlin Garland—a nearby gas station lad thought he was "some kind of politician when Iowa wasn't even that"—sits five dusty miles from Osage; each August the national Hobo Convention reconvenes at Britt; Clarion was the birthplace of the 4H emblem, in a country school inviting inspection; buffalo roam east of Nora Springs, and fossils can be found nearly everywhere if sought by the trained eye—all in an easy radius of Mason City, with all separated by miles of fresh air, open farmland, and wooded waterbeds a few miles apart.

Two lesser-known parks should be filled all summer, so restful yet intriguing is their terrain. The Wilkinson Pioneer Park, at Rock Falls, not only has a river for swimming and fishing and a covered bridge, it has a fish pond for 14-year-olds and under that jumps with stock that can't help but be caught. And the Shell Rock River Preserve, five miles east of Mason City, while hard to find, is a hidden gem for hikers and collectors.

Remember when Marion announced that all she wanted was a "plain man, a modest man, a decent man," and excluded "hand-kissing, wine-tasting silk pillas . . . or an Eagle, Odd Fellow, National Guardsman, Fire Chief, or Highlander, be he from the Arabian Nights or the French Foreign Legion"?

Well, that ought to be the welcome sign to north-central Iowa, for there is little to attract the dandy to this plain, modest, decent land with Marion's quiet, surprising moments of beauty. It's no fluke that this is the "land of *The Music Man*," where yesterday's virtues and vices outshine the newfangled gasoline automobiles and big-city ways. It's a refreshing change of pace to cross the footbridge at Willow Creek, lift your trombone high, and strut in person to that "high-stepping tune that races a man's heart as it marches majestically over the countryside."

————■————

Appendix B

MASON CITY? SHHHH. JUST KEEP IT UNDER YOUR CORNBELT

by Gordon Lee Burgett

(as submitted to the *Washington Post* for use in the travel section in 1974)

You can almost hear and see a high-stepping, brass-buttoned marching band triumphantly—if a bit atonally—cross that footbridge and sound those unforgettable opening notes of "Seventy-Six Trombones," for River City, U.S.A., is alive and throbbing in the heart of America's cornbelt.

It's really Mason City, a tree-lined main street of 32,000 in north-central Iowa, and it's where Meredith Willson (with two "l's," mind you) grew up, premiered musically one Wednesday afternoon before the Kiwanis Club at the still-operating Cerro Gordo Hotel, and left to play piccolo with Sousa and flute with Toscanini.

For most, Iowa ranks low on their "must see" list during vacation or travel time. Yet Mason City and environs put the logic of those lists to wonder. Particularly if you, like I, followed Harold Hill's every talk-song, scheme, and step from entrance to exit, hummed with the Buffalo Bills for months, and just knew that the locals, even in 1912, weren't going to buy his instruments sight unseen or tune untested.

Remember the root of all that trouble in River City, that billiards hall called the Pleazol (that's right, a billiards hall in River City!)? Well, if you doubt that the musical is a joyous well of childhood memories spilled over, stroll north on Federal Avenue from Central Park on the west side of the street and watch the sidewalk. What appears but a marble plate clearly announcing the original PLEAZOL! (Trouble has moved a few doors away, if billiards be the culprit; the old Pleazol is now a bar!)

You'll have to hunt a bit harder to find the Willson home (now in other private hands), but a guess using the Chamber of Commerce map will get you close. (It's green, five houses north of Willow Creek on the west side of Pennsylvania Avenue: please don't scare the dog.) Remember Marion the Librarian? In spirit she was Meredith's mother, and the old library, a few blocks away, now houses the Iowa Kempfer Mutual Insurance Company.

The most photographed landmark is the "Music Man" bridge, a movie-modeled version of a narrow overpass linking the town across Willow Creek. It's a few blocks east of the Willson home, past the new library and first-rate art museum. Between us, the original was actually found in East Park before it finally caved in, in 1950. A replica was rebuilt on that site, too, but the imitation at the end of Connecticut Avenue is so much more impressive—and nobody bothers to tell the visitors the truth.

Everywhere else you look, tucked between the

modern embellishments, are the old homes and haunts that magically reappeared on stage and screen. And if you wonder where the characters were drawn from, just look up on the front porches late any warm afternoon. Harold Hill? You needn't hunt in the graveyard. He was a composite, or as Willson himself said, "He's so many people I remember different ones every time I see the show." One person, though, stands clearly revealed from the presentations, that 10-year-old boy named Winthrop. That was Meredith Willson, and River City was Mason City in 1912 as he saw it then, or recalled seeing it, some 45 years later.

Since that year another local distinction took place. Frank Lloyd Wright's students put their architectural genius to work, and both at Rock Glen and at the Park Inn Hotel, at Central Park, the unique style is seen in half a dozen still-exciting structures.

Twice a year you'll be drawn nostalgically back to "The Land of the Music Man," although that was not originally planned. Each June, usually the second Tuesday (after school and just before haying), a hundred high school bands fill the streets and parks for a day of oompahpahing, while queen hopefuls nervously smile, hoping to become Miss North Iowa.

If you think that bands are unimportant today in mid-America, then you'll be surprised to find a third of the schools' students in uniform as musicians, flag girls, pom-pom squads, drum majors and majorettes, or ramrod-stiff standard-bearers, plumed and shining, all lining up eagerly to join the "big brass band" that puts a tingle in every spine at the end of that exciting day. Mason City fills up that Tuesday, so reservations at the motels are a must weeks before.

In 1953, Willson returned to lead the combined units in a 100-band celebration of Mason City's centennial. After the musical swept Broadway, he returned to new cheers in 1958. Ten years later it was the same electric thrill, but most vivid in everybody's memory was 1962, when Meredith not only led the grand finale, he drew bands from clear across the country.

In 1976, to the blast of as many trombones, if all goes as planned, the same Meredith Willson will be back again, perhaps for the last time, to celebrate our nation's bicentennial in "River City, U.S.A."

In March, another touch of old America, a la the Buffalo Bills, is seen in the River City Barbershop Annual Parade of Quartets. August features the Northern Iowa Fair.

Would you expect to find acres of wilderness, deep clear creeks teeming with bass and muskie, camping facilities in almost every town, and scores of half-known, well-tended county and township parks tucked into barely accessible crannies where you can spend a delightful weekend almost alone? Within 20 miles or so of Mason City are a dozen or so parks that bear investigation.

In fact, only eight miles west of the city is the most popular outdoor attraction in northern Iowa, a 6-by-2½ mile body of water appropriately called Clear Lake. It sits 100 feet higher than the surrounding countryside, like a tiny volcano, and long before tents of plastic came, the Sioux and Winnebago Indians spent summers there.

Now, thanks to a sanitary sewer that rims the state's third-largest body of water, it yields abundant stocks of muskie, walleye, northern pike, bass, and perch, while hunting at Ventura Marsh, to the west, reaps geese (Canada and snow), ducks, pheasant, even deer. The resort-like area is filled all year, with ice fishing, parachute-sailing (behind snowmobiles), and snowmobiling itself popular in the winter. The key time to visit is the Fourth of July, when the largest celebration in the state is held.

Campers can actually stay in Mason City's East Park, where 150 sites exist, tightly packed but with all facilities. Even more comfortable sites can be found only a few miles away.

Once you arrive there's a lot to do and see, and the people are as open as the terrain. The folks even smile. I almost broke out laughing when a freckle-faced lad in dungarees and bare feet yelled "howdy." Then he jumped on a motorcycle with a New Jersey license plate!

GLOSSARY

All rights. The publication purchases all rights to the item in its submitted form. To sell it again, the writer must rewrite it.

B/w's. Black and white photographs. Also *b & w's.*

Caption sheet. Sheet containing a description of the subject matter of the photographs, proofs, or slides that accompany it.

Contact sheets. See *proof sheets.*

Cover letter. Letter accompanying manuscripts or other submissions that explains their content or related information. Often sent with reprints, newspaper travel, and simultaneous submissions.

8 × 10s. Black and white glossy photographs that size (in inches!).

Feasibility study. A pre-query investigation to see whether it is feasible to research, write, and/or sell an article or book about a chosen subject.

First rights. The publication buys the right to have the copy appear on its pages first. Often called *first serial (periodical) rights.*

Freelancer. A writer who is not under contract for regular work or who sells his writings to different buyers.

Go-ahead. A positive reply to a query letter telling the writer to "go ahead and send the manuscript," implying that the editor will seriously review it for possible use and payment. Unless stated otherwise, the submission is on speculation.

In-flight. Publications made available on or by commercial airlines.

Kill fee. Fee for an assigned article that was ultimately not purchased.

Pix. Pictures: photographs or slides. Also *pics*.

Proof sheet. Negatives are laid in strips on a sheet of contact paper and the entire roll is developed, with each proof the size of the negative. Also called *contact sheets*. (These can also be made of single shots or in color.)

Query. A letter to an editor to elicit his interest in an article or book that the writer wants to write and sell to his publication or firm.

Reprint rights. See *second rights*.

Rewrite. Revision of a published manuscript, often expanding on one aspect of the subject.

SASE. Self-addressed stamped envelope sent with a query letter or manuscript to increase the likelihood that it will be returned.

Second rights. Publication buys the nonexclusive right to use an article that has already appeared in print. Second rights covers all such reuse; there are no third or subsequent rights. Can be sold to many publications simultaneously. Also called *reprint rights*.

Simultaneous submission. Submission of the same piece to more than one publication at the same time.

Stringer. A person who submits freelance copy from a fixed location or area.

Syndication. Selling articles or features through an organization for publication in many periodicals, often simultaneously. A writer can also syndicate his own material instead of working through a syndicate.

Tear sheet. A printed copy of a published work.

INDEX

Index

transitional paragraph, 77, 141–142
translations, 167
travel, 29, 32, 45–46, 137, 192
travel costs, 192
Travel and Leisure, 103, 201–203, 208
Travel Magazine, 151, 153–154, 201–203, 208–209
Travel Writer's Handbook, 30–31
TV/radio, 4, 165
typewriter, 146

unsolicited submissions, 6, 11–12
U.S.A. Today, 29

Wall Street Journal, 29

Washington Post, 120, 122, 154, 213, 216
whales, 168, 172, 175–179
widow lines, 147
word play, 141
word processor, 187–188
Working Press of the Nation, 33
working question, 139
Writer's Digest, 88
writer's guidelines, 125
Writer's Market, 11, 14, 20, 31, 36, 46, 48, 60, 64–65, 67–68, 75–76, 84–85, 88, 95, 113–114, 125–126, 144, 153, 166, 201, 208–209
writing, 23, 27, 67, 139–148, 212–213
writing feasibility, 72

OTHER BOOKS FROM THE
GORDON BURGETT LIBRARY

Gordon Burgett books and audiocassette tapes have helped tens of thousands of writers and speakers prosper. Here are his hand-picked titles selected especially for readers of this book.

BOOKS

Self-Publishing to Tightly-Targeted Markets

Subtitled "How to Earn $50,000 from Your First Book—Then Double It!", this book shows you how to identify and reach buyers who need specific information and are willing to pay almost anything to get it. Includes all you need to know, from book production to marketing. $14.95

Empire-Building by Writing and Speaking

If you have an exciting idea, you can have power—provided you learn how to increase your sphere of influence through writing and speaking. By widening your circle of influence, your income will multiply, sometimes a hundred times. Here are all the techniques necessary to take your idea, seminar, or expertise and make it your guide to a six- or even a seven-figure income. $15.95

Query Letters/Cover Letters

This famous book is the best guide to writing exciting query and cover letters—the kind that sell articles. This book has been hailed by *Booklist*: "For new writers or experienced ones looking for ways to multiply return on their work, this manual is highly recommended." $12.95

Ten Sales from One Article Idea

"Burgett has written a precise, step-by-step blueprint for getting published, one that even the novice ought to use with expectation of success . . . a valuable addition to any writer's library." *Palos Verdes View* (CA) $9.95

AUDIOCASSETTES

Here are the recordings of some of Gordon Burgett's own seminars before an audience of his students. If they include areas of interest to you, you will find them of immense and permanent value as you listen to them again and again.

Writing Travel Articles that Sell! (3 tapes) $39.95

Before You Write Your Nonfiction Book
   (3 tapes) $39.95

Writing Comedy Greeting Cards That Sell
   (2 tapes) $24.95

How to Set Up and Market Your Own Seminar
   (3 tapes) $44.95

Also Available From Prima Publishing

The Insider's Guide to Book Editors and Publishers by *Jeff Herman*

Updated annually. Here is the most comprehensive listing of book publishers and the names of editors and their specialty within each publishing house. Over 150 houses are included as well as the most complete information by top experts on what it takes to be successfully published. (hardcover) $27.95

And don't forget to order additional copies of
How to Sell More Than 75% of Your Freelance Writing. $12.95

ORDER FORM

Please send me the following items:

Quantity	Title	Unit Price	Total
_____	_____	$_____	$_____
_____	_____	$_____	$_____
_____	_____	$_____	$_____
_____	_____	$_____	$_____
_____	_____	$_____	$_____
		Subtotal	$_____

6.25% SALES TAX (California only) .... $_____

SHIPPING ($2 for the first item, $1 for each
additional volume) .... $_____

TOTAL ORDER .... $_____

_____

HOW TO ORDER

By telephone: With Visa/MC, call (916) 624-5718, Mon.–Fri.,
9–4 PST.

By Mail: Just fill out the information below and send with your
remittance.

I am paying by (check one): ☐ Check ☐ Money Order
☐ Visa/MC

My name is _____

I live at _____

City _____ State _____ Zip _____

Visa/MC # _____ Exp. _____

Signature _____

PRIMA PUBLISHING
P.O. Box 1260B7
Rocklin, CA 95677
(Satisfaction unconditionally guaranteed)